# ETERNAL JUDGEMENT

## Michael E.B. Maher

Unless otherwise indicated, all Scripture quotations in this teaching are from the *New King James Version* of the bible.

Revised Edition 2017

**ISBN:** 978-0-620-77566-3

# Books by Michael E.B. Maher

*Born Free from Sin*
*Repentance from Dead Works*
*Faith Toward God*
*Doctrine of Baptisms*
*Laying on of Hands*
*Resurrection of the Dead*
*The Will of Man*
*The Spirit of Man*
*The Conscience of Man*
*The Mind of Man*
*The Body of Man*
*Spiritual Gifts*
*The Revelation Gifts*
*The Power Gifts*
*Ministry Gifts*
*There is Sin to Death*
*Prayer*
*Of Such is the Kingdom*
*Overcoming Unforgiveness*
*The Two Gospels Explained*
*Being led by the Spirit*

# Contents

# Chapter 1
## Our eternal decision

### Introduction

*Hebrews 5:12-14 "For though by this time you ought to be teachers, you need someone to teach you again the first principles of the oracles of God; and you have come to need milk and not solid food. (13) For everyone who partakes only of milk is unskilled in the word of righteousness, for he is a babe. (14) But solid food belongs to those who are of full age, that is, those who by reason of use have their senses exercised to discern both good and evil."*

*Hebrews 6:1-2 "Therefore, leaving the discussion of the elementary principles of Christ, let us go on to perfection, not laying again the foundation of repentance from dead works and of faith toward God, (2) of the doctrine of baptisms, of laying on of hands, of resurrection of the dead, and of eternal judgment."*

There are six foundational doctrines to the Christian faith. Because they are foundational, every believer should have a clear understanding of each one of these doctrines, and live by them. Those who have a clear understanding of these doctrines and who also live by them, will have a sure foundation. And they will not be deceived by any false teachings, that they may come across in their Christian walk. Scripture reveals to us that these doctrines are the milk of God's word, which all new born believers should feed on. However, even mature adults drink milk as part of their natural diet. In the spirit, that principle remains the same. And so, it is good for mature believers to also revisit the foundational principles of Christ from time to time, to ensure that their foundations remain solid. In this teaching, we will examine the doctrine of eternal judgement, which is the last of the six foundational doctrines taught to the body of Christ. Sadly, this particular doctrine is not understood very well, mainly because it is very rarely ever taught in the church. For varied reasons, ministers of the gospel stay away from teaching this doctrine. As an illustration, let me give you an example of what happened to me recently. I was at a men's breakfast, and I shared a small five-minute truth about the eternal judgement of believers. No sooner had I sat down, then one of the pastors quickly stood up and made the following comment, "Folks let's not get all depressed, for the gospel is good news. We know there is a judgement but it's all good news, because were all saved". I think this pastor's comment about sums it up. Ministers stay away from this doctrine because they find it depressing. And they also have a warped understanding of the doctrine, because they believe that being saved is all that matters. If being saved is all that matters, then why does our Lord list eternal judgement as being one of His foundation doctrines, that He wants every believer to have a clear understanding of? Because ministers neglect this doctrine, many believers are not even aware that they will be judged. In this life, people who invest wisely for their retirement, enjoy the fruits of their investments when they retire. However, there are many who never invest for their

# Our eternal decision

retirement, and just hope for the best. So, what about our eternal inheritance? Should we not be even more wise in investing for eternity? And yet so many believers approach eternity, just hoping for the best. We will see in this teaching, that our Lord Jesus does not view that as being wise.

## We must endure to the end

*1 Corinthians 11:30-32 "For this reason many are weak and sick among you, and many sleep. (31) For if we would judge ourselves, we would not be judged. (32) But when we are judged, we are chastened by the Lord, that we may not be condemned with the world."*

*Romans 11:17-22 "And if some of the branches were broken off, and you, being a wild olive tree, were grafted in among them, and with them became a partaker of the root and fatness of the olive tree, (18) do not boast against the branches. But if you do boast, remember that you do not support the root, but the root supports you. (19) You will say then, "Branches were broken off that I might be grafted in." (20) Well said. Because of unbelief they were broken off, and you stand by faith. Do not be haughty, but fear. (21) For if God, did not spare the natural branches, He may not spare you either. (22) Therefore, consider the goodness and severity of God: on those who fell, severity; but toward you, goodness, if you continue in His goodness. Otherwise you also will be cut off."*

# Our eternal decision

*Revelation 3:16-19 "So then, because you are lukewarm, and neither cold nor hot, I will vomit you out of My mouth. (17) Because you say, 'I am rich, have become wealthy, and have need of nothing'-and do not know that you are wretched, miserable, poor, blind, and naked-- (18) I counsel you to buy from Me gold refined in the fire, that you may be rich; and white garments, that you may be clothed, that the shame of your nakedness may not be revealed; and anoint your eyes with eye salve, that you may see. (19) As many as I love, I rebuke and chasten. Therefore, be zealous and repent."*

Before we go any further on the subject of eternal judgement, we need to deal with the erroneous teaching that has caused many believers to stumble. Because we are dealing with eternity in this teaching, it is of vital importance that we deal with this particular issue. The false teaching that I am referring to, is that once someone is saved they can never lose their salvation. In other words, once someone has made the decision to accept Jesus Christ as their Lord and Saviour, that decision can never be reversed. All believers still have their free will after they are saved, and so to say that they cannot reverse their decision cannot be true. Some will argue that one who is born again, will never want to reverse their decision to have Jesus as their Lord. If that is the case, then why does our Lord Jesus judge certain believers so that they will not be condemned with the world? In writing to believers in first Corinthians chapter eleven quoted above, the Holy Spirit reveals to us that our Lord judges some believers in this life. Why does He do that? Scripture tells us that He does that because He is concerned about our eternal destination. And so, when He sees that if we were to continue down a certain path that will lead us to being condemned with the world, He then judges us in this life, rather than allowing us to be eternally condemned. The Holy Spirit through the apostle Paul, in writing to the church in Rome quoted above, warns us as believers, that if we choose not to continue in the goodness of God, that He will cut us off just as natural Israel have been cut off. Clearly, Christians can make the decision not to continue in God's goodness, otherwise the Holy Spirit would never have written this warning to us. When our Lord Jesus wrote to the church in Laodicea as quoted above, He told them that unless they turned around from the path that they were on, that He would eventually vomit them out of His mouth. In other words, they would no longer be in the body of Christ. And so, we see that scripture plainly teaches us that it is certainly possible for believers to reverse their decision to accept the Lordship of Jesus, and the Lord warns us about this. I also want you to notice that in all three scriptures quoted above, the Holy Spirit was writing to born again believers. Some who teach falsely that no one can lose their salvation, claim that people that fall away were never really saved to begin with. However, the Lord Jesus and the Holy Spirit know the difference between those who are saved and those who are not saved. And in these scriptures, they are warning those who are saved.

*1 John 5:16 "If anyone sees his brother sinning a sin not to death, he will ask, and He will give him life for those who commit sin not to death. There is sin to death. I do not say that he should pray about that."*

*James 1:14-15 "But each one is tempted when he is drawn away by his own desires and enticed. (15) Then, when desire has conceived, it gives birth to sin; and sin, when it is full-grown, brings forth death."*

*John 3:18 "He who believes in Him is not condemned; but he who does not believe is condemned already, because he has not believed in the name of the only begotten Son of God."*

In the passage of scripture from first John chapter five quoted above, the apostle John refers to two types of sin that believers can commit. He refers to sin not to death, and he tells us that we can pray for forgiveness for the believer who commits this sin and that the Lord will forgive those sins. But he also refers to sin to death, and he tells us that we cannot pray for forgiveness for the believer who commits this sin. The reason we cannot pray for this sin, is because there is no forgiveness for this sin. So, what is the sin to death? In James chapter one quoted above, the Holy Spirit reveals to us that when sin is full-grown, it brings forth death. James is writing to believers when he tells them that if they are to continue in sin, that it will eventually lead to their death. The death that he is referring to, is spiritual death not physical death. What James is saying is that all sin left unchecked, will eventually lead the believer to committing the sin to death that John spoke about. We saw earlier in the passage of scripture from Corinthians, that Jesus judges us so that we will not be condemned with the world. What does that mean? It cannot mean that as a result of any sin we have committed, that we will be condemned with the world. Because every Christian falls into the category of committing sin from time to time. As revealed to us in John chapter three above, there is really only one sin for which the world will be condemned. And that is the sin of rejecting Jesus Christ. Knowing what sin the world will be condemned for, gives us a bit more insight into what our Lord Jesus wants to save us from, by judging us in this life. He knows that if we continue down the path of sin left unchecked, that we will eventually commit the sin to death. And that sin is the sin of rejecting Jesus as Lord.

*Galatians 6:1 "Brethren, if a man is overtaken in any trespass, you who are spiritual restore such a one in a spirit of gentleness, considering yourself lest you also be tempted."*

*Revelation 2:20-23 "Nevertheless I have a few things against you, because you allow that woman Jezebel, who calls herself a prophetess, to teach and seduce My servants to commit sexual immorality and eat things sacrificed to idols. (21) And I gave her time to repent of her sexual immorality, and she did not repent. (22) Indeed, I will cast her into a sickbed, and those who commit adultery with her into great tribulation, unless they repent of their deeds. (23) I will kill her children with death, and all the churches shall know that I am He who searches the minds and hearts. And I will give to each one of you according to your works."*

We saw earlier in first John, that if we see any brother in the Lord committing sin, that we should pray for that brother. The reason we pray, is so that the Lord will forgive them their sin and restore them to righteousness. We are not to condemn them, we are to pray for them. How many believers do you know that practice this? And then the Holy Spirit reveals to us in Galatians quoted above, that those of us who are spiritual, should restore the Christian who is sinning. And we are to do so in a spirit of gentleness, not condemnation. The book of Revelation quoted above, gives us a vivid account of how our Lord deals with believers that continue in sin. In the church at Thyatira there was a believer who was obviously deluded into thinking that she was called by the Lord to be a prophetess. That church had allowed her to teach, and she had a following in that church. Over time, because she had been allowed to continue teaching, even though our Lord had not called her to the ministry, she had started to teach more and more false doctrine, to the point that she was now even teaching fellow believers to commit sexual immorality and eat things offered to idols. Our Lord tells us that He had given her time to repent and that she had not repented, and that now He would judge her and her followers with sickness and tribulation. He then tells us that if she and her followers still refused to repent, that He would then eventually judge them with physical death. He did all of this so that these believers would not be condemned with the world. The above example has illustrated to us just how the Lord judges those who refuse to judge themselves. This is a clear example of that which Paul spoke about, to the church at Corinth. For you will recall that we saw earlier that they were also judged with weakness, sickness and eventually physical death. When we see believers, who become ill and we see believers who die early deaths, we sometimes ask how it is that our Lord Jesus allowed these tragedies to come upon them? Sometimes the reason for these events taking place in the lives of believers, is because they have not judged themselves. And so, our Lord Jesus has stepped in and judged them. I need to clarify that not all sin will be judged by the Lord with physical death, only those sins that will eventually lead the believer to committing the sin to death. We have seen that our Lord first gives us time to repent. If after a while, we refuse to judge ourselves and repent of our sin, then He allows sickness and tribulation to come upon us. If we still refuse to judge ourselves and repent of our sin, even in our sickness and tribulation, then He will eventually judge us with physical death. He does all of this so that we will not reach the stage of committing the sin to death, and thus be condemned with the world.

*Hebrews 3:12-14 "Beware, brethren, lest there be in any of you an evil heart of unbelief in departing from the living God; (13) but exhort one another daily, while it is called "TODAY," lest any of you be hardened through the deceitfulness of sin. (14) For we have become partakers of Christ if we hold the beginning of our confidence steadfast to the end."*

*Hebrews 6:4-6 "For it is impossible for those who were once enlightened, and have tasted the heavenly gift, and have become partakers of the Holy Spirit, (5) and have tasted the good word of God and the powers of the age to come, (6) if they fall away, to renew them again to repentance, since they crucify again for themselves the Son of God, and put Him to an open shame."*

*2 Timothy 2:12 "If we endure, we shall also reign with Him. If we deny Him, He also will deny us."*

However, not every believer who refuses to repent of their sin, is judged by the Lord with physical death. Some are allowed by the Lord to continue on their path of sin, and they eventually do commit the sin to death. It may be that these believers do not have other believers praying for them, and so our Lord is unable to intervene in their lives. Pray for believers when you see them in sin. They need your prayers, for they have become blind to their sin. And those of you who are spiritual, restore your brothers in a spirit of gentleness. Their eternity is at stake. So how is it possible that one who has accepted Jesus as their Lord and Saviour would ever reach a stage where they are willing to reject Him as their Lord? In Hebrews chapter three quoted above, the Holy Spirit teaches us that sin has the effect of hardening the heart of the believer. A believer's heart that becomes sufficiently hardened through sin, will eventually depart from the living God. In this passage of scripture, the Holy Spirit is warning believers about the effects of sin, He is not warning unbelievers. In Hebrews chapter six quoted above, the Holy Spirit describes the condition of believers who have turned their backs on following Jesus as their Lord. In other words, they have reversed their decision to follow after Christ. These believers have allowed their hearts to become hardened through sin, and they have become so backslidden, that serving Christ no longer interests them. They have denied Jesus as their Lord and there is no way back for them. (For a more detailed teaching on this subject see my book "There is Sin to Death"). The point remains clear. Once you have made the eternal decision to accept Jesus Christ as your Lord and Saviour, you must guard that decision by holding the beginning of your confidence steadfast to the end of your time here on the planet. Those who endure to the end, will reign with Him. Those who deny Him will be denied by Him.

## Our eternal decision

*2 Peter 3:13 "Nevertheless we, according to His promise, look for new heavens and a new earth in which righteousness dwells."*

*Revelation 20:13-15 "The sea gave up the dead who were in it, and Death and Hades delivered up the dead who were in them. And they were judged, each one according to his works. (14) Then Death and Hades were cast into the lake of fire. This is the second death. (15) And anyone not found written in the Book of Life was cast into the lake of fire."*

God dwells in eternity. We, even as believers, have a very limited understanding of eternity. In this present age, when every person leaves this planet, we all go to one of two places. We either go to heaven, or we go to hell. Those who have accepted Christ Jesus as Lord and Saviour go to heaven, while those who have not accepted Jesus as Lord go to hell. But heaven and hell are not man's final destinations. Both places are temporary stopovers, on our way to our final destinations. Even though some have already been in those temporary stopovers for six thousand years and longer, they are still just waiting for their eternal destinations. Adam's second son Abel, has been resting in heaven for well over six thousand years. While his older brother Cain, who murdered him, has been reserved under punishment in hell for a similar period of time. This gives us just a little glimpse into what eternity is like. You say, what is man's final destination then? As quoted from two Peter chapter three above, the Holy Spirit reveals to us that those who are currently resting in heaven, are destined to dwell with God in the new earth that He is still to create. And as revealed to us in Revelation chapter twenty quoted above, those who are currently waiting in hell, are destined to be taken out on the last day, to be cast for all eternity into the lake which burns with fire and brimstone. Where one is destined for, after they leave this planet is for all eternity, there are no second chances. And so, we see that what we do in our very short time on earth, impacts our eternal destiny. In fact, our eternal destination is determined by only one decision that we make. And that decision is to either accept or reject, Jesus Christ as our Lord and Saviour. That decision can also only be made while we are alive on the planet, and everyone has opportunity right up until the time they draw their last breath, to make that decision. If we choose to receive salvation through Jesus Christ, then we are born again. And once we are born again we have passed from death to life, and we are destined for our eternal home in God's new earth. For those who choose to reject salvation through Jesus Christ, they remain spiritually dead and are destined for the eternal torment of the lake of fire and brimstone.

# Our eternal decision

*2 Timothy 4:1 "I charge you therefore before God and the Lord Jesus Christ, who will judge the living and the dead at His appearing and His kingdom."*

*John 5:28-29 "Do not marvel at this; for the hour is coming in which all who are in the graves will hear His voice (29) and come forth-- those who have done good, to the resurrection of life, and those who have done evil, to the resurrection of condemnation."*

And so, we see that our eternal destination is determined by the one crucial decision that we all make while on the earth. But there is more to it than that. Although the one decision we make determines where we will be for eternity, it is not that decision that determines how each of us will spend eternity in our final destination. That is where eternal judgement comes in. There is coming a day in which each one of us, believer and unbeliever alike, will be judged. In second Timothy chapter four quoted above, the Holy Spirit reveals that everyone will be judged by the Lord Jesus on that day. The living that He refers to are the believers, while the dead that He refers to, are the unbelievers. Our short lives on this planet will be judged in perfect detail and absolute impartiality. The result of that judgement for the believer, will determine their place and inheritance in God's kingdom for the rest of eternity. And the result of that judgement for the unbeliever, will determine the degree of torment that they will suffer in the lake of fire for all eternity. Our Lord Jesus linked His judgment to the resurrection of the dead at the end of the age. Notice that our Lord refers to two resurrections. The first, He calls the resurrection of life, which is the resurrection of His saints. The second, He calls the resurrection of condemnation, which is the resurrection of the unbelievers.

# Chapter 2
# The saints' judgement
## The saints will not be condemned

*John 5:24 "Most assuredly, I say to you, he who hears My word and believes in Him who sent Me has everlasting life, and shall not come into judgment, but has passed from death into life."*

*John 3:16-18 "For God so loved the world that He gave His only begotten Son, that whoever believes in Him should not perish but have everlasting life. (17) For God, did not send His Son into the world to condemn the world, but that the world through Him might be saved. (18) "He who believes in Him is not condemned; but he who does not believe is condemned already, because he has not believed in the name of the only begotten Son of God."*

*1 Corinthians 6:12 "All things are lawful for me, but all things are not helpful. All things are lawful for me, but I will not be brought under the power of any."*

The saints will not be judged with regards to salvation, for we have already passed from death into life. Jesus taught us that we as believers, have eternal life and we will not be judged. The judgement that Jesus is referring to in John chapter five quoted above, is the righteous judgement of God that all unbelievers will incur on their day of judgement. This is the judgement that all unbelievers will incur when they are raised from the dead on the last day. We will look at the judgement of the unbelievers later in this teaching. In John chapter three quoted above, our Lord Jesus has made it very clear that those who believe in Him will not be condemned, and thus perish with the world, for they have received everlasting life. And so, the point remains that once we have believed in Jesus as our Lord and Saviour, we have passed from death to life and we are no longer subject to the unbeliever's judgement of condemnation. Jesus Christ died for our sins, and all that He requires of us to be saved, is simply to believe in Him and confess Him as Lord. When we do this, our spirits are born-again and we are made alive in Christ. The gift that we receive from God is eternal life, and so our spirits can no longer die. We have become as the angels of God in this respect, for they too can never die. However, as we have already seen in the previous chapter, there is one sin that the believer can commit, that will cause their spirits to die. And that is the sin to death. Every other sin committed by the believer, cannot affect the spirit of the believer. The reason for this is because under the new covenant, we are under grace. Under grace, all things are lawful to the believer. This truth is revealed to us by the Holy Spirit in first Corinthians chapter six quoted above. If there was anything that was not lawful to the believer, then the moment that law was transgressed, the spirit of the believer would die. You will recall that when Adam and Eve sinned, their spirits died immediately. The reason their spirits died immediately, was because they were not under grace. And so, the moment they transgressed, judgement was pronounced, and they died spiritually.

*1 Peter 2:15-16 "For this is the will of God, that by doing good you may put to silence the ignorance of foolish men-- (16) as free, yet not using liberty as a cloak for vice, but as bondservants of God."*

*Galatians 6:7-8 "Do not be deceived, God is not mocked; for whatever a man sows, that he will also reap. (8) For he who sows to his flesh will of the flesh reap corruption, but he who sows to the Spirit will of the Spirit reap everlasting life."*

But under the new covenant, it is no longer the case that sin is immediately judged with spiritual death. For we read earlier in James chapter one, that now sin must become full grown, before it produces spiritual death. In other words, under the new covenant there is a grace period given to the believer who sins. During this grace period, even though the believer may be walking in unrepentant sin, that sin does not impact their spirits. And their spirits remain alive unto God. Foolishly, some have taken this truth of grace and used it as a license to commit sin, not realising that they are then on the path to committing the sin to death. For notice that Paul states in one Corinthians quoted above, that even though all things were lawful for him, he would not allow himself to be brought under the power of any. You will recall that our Lord Jesus taught us that the one who commits sin, becomes a slave of sin. That is what Paul was referring to, when he stated that he would not allow himself to be brought under the power of anything. Even though because he was under grace, there was no sin that he could commit that would affect his spirit, Paul understood that to commit sin was to give sin power over him. Satan's aim is to kill the believer, and he knows that sin will get the job done. For the wages of sin is death. As long as Satan can get the believer to commit sin, he now has power over that believer to lead him down the path to eventually committing the sin to death. The Holy Spirit through the apostle Peter as quoted in first Peter chapter two above, warns believers not to use the liberty that we have under grace, to live in sin. The grace that we are under in the new covenant is there to bring us to repentance, if we do sin. For it is the goodness of God that leads us to repentance. For those believers who abuse the grace of God and continue to live in sin, the Holy Spirit tells us plainly in Galatians chapter six quoted above, that God is not mocked. A believer who continues to sow to their flesh, will reap the wages of sin, which is death. The word translated "corruption" also mean to perish. There are two deaths that sin can produce in the lives of believers, who continue to live in sin. The one is physical death and the other is spiritual death. The physical death that I am referring to here, is early death. For until the Lord returns, we will all eventually die physically. But these believers who are judged with physical death, do not live out their full time on the earth, and are taken to be with the Lord earlier than God intended for their lives. If physical death is reaped first, then those believers will go to be with the Lord Jesus when they die. The reason for that, is because their spirits are still alive unto God, and they still have the eternal life of God in them. However, if spiritual death is reaped first, then those believers will go to hell when they die, for they would have already committed the sin to death. It is by the grace of God, that many of these believers reap physical death before they ever get to the place where they can commit the sin of reaping spiritual death. But as we have seen in the previous chapter, this is not always the case. And there are believers who reap spiritual death first. Sin is not to be taken lightly, as it can carry eternal consequences. You can therefore readily see just how dangerous the false doctrine of "once saved, always saved", is.

*1 Corinthians 5:1-5 "It is actually reported that there is sexual immorality among you, and such sexual immorality as is not even named among the Gentiles--that a man has his father's wife! (2) And you are puffed up, and have not rather mourned, that he who has done this deed might be taken away from among you. (3) For I indeed, as absent in body but present in spirit, have already judged (as though I were present) him who has so done this deed. (4) In the name of our Lord Jesus Christ, when you are gathered together, along with my spirit, with the power of our Lord Jesus Christ, (5) deliver such a one to Satan for the destruction of the flesh, that his spirit may be saved in the day of the Lord Jesus."*

*1 Corinthians 11:30-32 "For this reason many are weak and sick among you, and many sleep. (31) For if we would judge ourselves, we would not be judged. (32) But when we are judged, we are chastened by the Lord, that we may not be condemned with the world."*

In one Corinthians chapter five quoted above, the Holy Spirit gives us a clear account of a believer being judged with early death, because they are continuing in sin. In this account, the believer in question was living in the unrepentant sin of adultery. The apostle Paul, pronounced judgement on this individual, by handing him over to Satan for the destruction of his flesh. There were two reasons that this was done. The one reason was to remove the contaminating influence of sin, from the church. The second reason that this was done, and this is the point we want to concentrate on in this teaching, was so that this believer's salvation would still be intact on the day of the Lord Jesus. What the Holy Spirit reveals to us in this passage of scripture, is that if this believer had not been taken to be with the Lord, then he would have eventually reached the point of committing the sin to death, and he would have lost his salvation. And so even though this believer would die while practicing the sin of adultery, his salvation was still assured. And he would not be condemned with the world. The reason for that was because his spirit was still alive unto God. It still had the eternal life of God in it, and it remained unaffected by the sin of adultery. Eternity is far more important to God, than this life. And as we have already seen in the previous chapter, the Lord will do whatever is necessary to ensure that all of His children spend eternity with Him. If needed, our Lord Jesus judges His church in this life. He does this, so that we can be kept from the judgement of condemnation, which will be incurred by the unbelievers on their day of judgement. In first Corinthians chapter eleven quoted above, the Holy Spirit is writing to believers, not unbelievers. The judgement that He is referring to in this passage, is the judgement that believers can expect in this life, if they refuse to repent of sin in their lives. In order to keep them from being condemned

# The saints' judgement

with the world, there are numerous ways in which the Lord Jesus judges His church in this life. One of those ways, is to take the believer to be with Him earlier than God originally intended for their lives. He does this if He sees that the path that the believer is on, will ultimately result in their committing the sin to death. And so, we can clearly see that believers will not be condemned with the world. Even those who die in unrepentant sin, will not be condemned with the world. The reason for that is because they are born-again, with the nature and life of God in their spirits, and their spirits are unaffected by sin.

## The saints will be judged

*Romans 14:10-12 "But why do you judge your brother? Or why do you show contempt for your brother? For we shall all stand before the judgment seat of Christ. (11) For it is written: "AS I LIVE, SAYS THE LORD, EVERY KNEE SHALL BOW TO ME, AND EVERY TONGUE SHALL CONFESS TO GOD." (12) So, then each of us shall give account of himself to God."*

*James 2:12-13 "So speak and so do as those who will be judged by the law of liberty. (13) For judgment is without mercy to the one who has shown no mercy. Mercy triumphs over judgment."*

*2 Corinthians 5:9-11 "Therefore we make it our aim, whether present or absent, to be well pleasing to Him. (10) For we must all appear before the judgment seat of Christ, that each one may receive the things done in the body, according to what he has done, whether good or bad. (11) Knowing, therefore, the terror of the Lord, we persuade men; but we are well known to God, and I also trust are well known in your consciences."*

And so, we have seen that believers will not experience the judgement of condemnation that unbelievers will incur, for we have already passed from death to life. But scripture also clearly tells us that we, as believers, will be judged. In Romans chapter fourteen quoted above, the scripture is speaking to us as believers, when it tells us that we will all stand before the judgement seat of Christ. As believers, we will not be judged with regards to salvation, for the blood of Jesus has already saved us. But it is our works, which we have done as believers, that will be judged on that day. The Holy Spirit clearly tells us that we will have to give an account of ourselves to our Lord Jesus, on that day. In James chapter two quoted above, the Holy Spirit through the apostle James, tells us that as believers, we are to conduct our lives on earth in a manner that will meet the required benchmark by which we will be judged. The benchmark that he refers to, is the law of liberty, which is the new covenant. I will not in this section, discuss the type of judgement that the believer will incur on that day, for we will discuss that in a bit more detail later in this teaching. But the fact that the Holy Spirit mentions that we need to be showing mercy to others in this life, so that we can expect to receive mercy on that day, gives us a little bit of insight as to what that judgement will be like. And again, in two Corinthians chapter five quoted above, the Holy Spirit through the apostle Paul, tells us that all believers should make it their aim to live lives that are well pleasing

# The saints' judgement

to the Lord. He says that the reason we should do this, is because we all must appear before the judgement seat of Christ, to receive the things we have done in this life. This passage of scripture is written to believers, not to unbelievers. Notice also, that in this passage of scripture that the Holy Spirit reveals to us that we will receive from the Lord what we have done in this life, both good and bad. Make no mistake, the believers judgement will be completely thorough and also completely impartial, for God shows favouritism to no man.

## We focus on the prize

*Hebrews 12:16-17 "lest there be any fornicator or profane person like Esau, who for one morsel of food sold his birthright. (17) For you know that afterward, when he wanted to inherit the blessing, he was rejected, for he found no place for repentance, though he sought it diligently with tears."*

*Luke 19:20-26 "Then another came, saying, 'Master, here is your mina, which I have kept put away in a handkerchief. (21) For I feared you, because you are an austere man. You collect what you did not deposit, and reap what you did not sow.' (22) And he said to him, 'Out of your own mouth I will judge you, you wicked servant. You knew that I was an austere man, collecting what I did not deposit and reaping what I did not sow. (23) Why then did you not put my money in the bank, that at my coming I might have collected it with interest?' (24) "And he said to those who stood by, 'Take the mina from him, and give it to him who has ten*

*minas.' (25) (But they said to him, 'Master, he has
ten minas.') (26) 'For I say to you, that to everyone
who has will be given; and from him who does not
have, even what he has will be taken away from
him."*

     I mentioned earlier, that our Lord Jesus does not
view the approach to our eternal judgement of just
"hoping for the best", as being wise. And yet most
believers approach their day of judgement with that exact
attitude, "Well I'll just hope for the best, and if I am
rewarded great, but if I miss out, then that's just too bad.
But at least I know I'm saved". Think about that attitude
for a moment. We are talking about our eternal destiny.
As a result of this judgement, it will be decided just how
we are to spend the rest of eternity in the kingdom of God.
In Hebrews chapter twelve quoted above, the Holy Spirit
gives us the account of Esau and his earthly inheritance. If
you read the account in the old testament, you will see
that Esau sold his birth right to his younger brother Jacob.
When Esau sold his birth right, all he was concerned
about, was his immediate needs. His future inheritance
was the furthest thing from his mind. He was hungry, and
when given the choice to give up his birth right in order to
satisfy his immediate needs, he chose his immediate needs
over his future inheritance. His actions had disastrous
consequences, because years later when the time came for
him to inherit the blessing, he was rejected. The scripture
reveals to us that even though he sought with tears, to find
a way to inherit the blessing, it was too late. Don't forget
that Esau was Isaac's favourite son. I'm sure that when
Esau made his choice, he must have had the thought that,
"I'm sure it will all turn out alright, because after all, I am

my Father's favourite son". But Isaac's hands were tied. Even though Esau was his favourite son, God held Esau accountable for his decision, and he could not receive the blessing. Esau's actions were an admonishment to us today, of how we are to treat our eternal inheritance. Many today, concentrate on this life and give no thought for their eternal inheritance. Their view is that Jesus loves them and He will take care of their inheritance for them. But they fail to realise that Jesus can only reward us for that which we have done according to the Father's will, on that day. To find out on that day, that you have not done the Father's will for your life will be too late, and your inheritance will be lost. The parable that our Lord taught us in Luke chapter fourteen quoted above, clearly illustrates this point. Some will have no inheritance on that day, because they chose not to do the will of the Father.

> *1 Corinthians 9:24-27 "Do you not know that those who run in a race all run, but one receives the prize? Run in such a way that you may obtain it. (25) And everyone who competes for the prize is temperate in all things. Now they do it to obtain a perishable crown, but we for an imperishable crown. (26) Therefore, I run thus: not with uncertainty. Thus, I fight: not as one who beats the air. (27) But I discipline my body and bring it into subjection, lest, when I have preached to others, I myself should become disqualified."*

> *Philippians 3:12-15 "Not that I have already attained, or am already perfected; but I press on, that I may lay hold of that for which Christ Jesus has*

*also laid hold of me. (13) Brethren, I do not count myself to have apprehended; but one thing I do, forgetting those things which are behind and reaching forward to those things which are ahead, (14) I press toward the goal for the prize of the upward call of God in Christ Jesus. (15) Therefore, let us, as many as are mature, have this mind; and if in anything you think otherwise, God will reveal even this to you."*

In one Corinthians chapter nine quoted above, the Holy Spirit through the apostle Paul, counsels us to approach our day of judgement with purpose. He likens it to competing in a race. He tells us that we should compete in such a manner, that we are determined to win that race. He tells us that an athlete who wants to win their race, trains and prepares with purpose. Think about Olympic athletes. They train for years and are completely focused on winning the gold medal in their chosen field. If we are to receive the crowns laid up in store for us on that day, then we must have that very same attitude in our Christian walk. Our eternal crowns are not received in any other way. In Philippians chapter three quoted above, the apostle Paul tells us that he presses toward the goal of the prize of the upward call of God in Christ Jesus. Again, the Holy Spirit puts the apostle Paul forward as an example to us, of just how focused we should be on attaining the eternal prize that is set before us. Notice that Paul tells us that this should be the attitude of mature believers. The reason that mature believers should have this attitude, is because they should have by this time, learnt to determine God's will for their lives. Baby Christians are still learning how to hear from God, and how to follow after the leading of the Holy Spirit. They do not yet know what God's will is for their lives. But with regards to mature believers, it should be different. Because they should by this time, have clearly heard from God as to what works He has prepared beforehand, for them to walk in. And having learnt from God, what it is that He has called them to do, they can now focus on completing that work.

*John 17:4-5 "I have glorified You on the earth. I have finished the work which You have given Me to do. (5) And now, O Father, glorify Me together with Yourself, with the glory which I had with You before the world was."*

*2 Timothy 4:7-8 "I have fought the good fight, I have finished the race, I have kept the faith. (8) Finally, there is laid up for me the crown of righteousness, which the Lord, the righteous Judge, will give to me on that Day, and not to me only but also to all who have loved His appearing."*

The Holy Spirit through the apostle Peter in first Peter chapter two, has told us that Christ Jesus is our example, and that we should follow in His footsteps. In John's gospel quoted above, our Lord Jesus was praying to the Father the night before He was to be crucified. Notice that the Lord Jesus stated that He had glorified God the Father on the earth. Jesus said that He did that, by completing the work that God the Father had given Him to do, on the earth. As a reward for finishing the Father's work on the earth, Jesus said that God would glorify Him together with God the Father. In other words, Jesus received His eternal reward from God the Father, because He had completed the work given to Him to do, by the Father. If the Son of God was glorified by the Father because of His obedience in finishing the work of the Father, then we are no different. If we are going to receive our eternal rewards from God our Father, then we too are going to have complete the work given to us by the Father. In second Timothy chapter four quoted above, Paul the apostle, tells us that he had finished his race and that he had kept the faith. When Paul wrote this letter to Timothy, his time on the earth was drawing to a close, and he would soon depart to be with the Lord Jesus. I want you to notice that Paul was very confident that he had completed the work that he had been given to do on the earth by the Lord. For he confidently stated that he had finished his race. You will recall earlier, that Paul likened his Christian walk to competing in a race. But also, notice that not only was Paul confident that he had completed his race, but he was just as assured that he would receive the reward of his crown from the Lord, on that day. In effect Paul was saying the same thing that Jesus said at the end of His time on the earth. Paul was saying that he had finished the work given to him by the Lord on the earth, and that he would receive the glory laid up for him in heaven, as a reward for his obedience. Every believer, when their time comes to leave this life to be with the Lord Jesus, should be able to make that self-same statement. For this is the will of the Lord Jesus for each one of His saints. Now compare that statement with the one I quoted earlier, "Well I'll just hope for the best, and if I am rewarded great, but if I miss out, then that's just too bad. But at least I know I'm saved". From the examples given to us by our Lord Jesus and the apostle Paul, you can readily see that this is not how our Lord wants us to approach our day of judgement.

*Romans 6:8 "Now if we died with Christ, we believe that we shall also live with Him."*

*Colossians 2:13-14 "And you, being dead in your trespasses and the uncircumcision of your flesh, He has made alive together with Him, having forgiven you all trespasses, (14) having wiped out the handwriting of requirements that was against us, which was contrary to us. And He has taken it out of the way, having nailed it to the cross."*

*2 Corinthians 5:17 "Therefore, if anyone is in Christ, he is a new creation; old things have passed away; behold, all things have become new."*

We read earlier in Philippians, that Paul stated that he deliberately chose to forget those things that were behind him. Paul had learnt to forget everything from his past life, because it counted for nothing in the kingdom of God. When Paul made this comment, he was referring to his life before he was saved. Even though Paul had achieved more than most of his countrymen, in his walk as an ultra-orthodox Jew, he counted all of that as rubbish for the sake of gaining Christ. No believer will reach their goal in Christ, by constantly looking at the past which is behind them. We need to view our lives now as heaven does, and look forward to the goal set before us in Christ Jesus. As far as heaven is concerned, everything done by the believer prior to them being born-again, no longer exists. Because the person that lived before that time has in fact died, as revealed to us in Romans chapter six quoted above. And everything that they ever did, is completely erased as if that life never existed. Many believers do not walk in this reality. When you talk to them, they talk about their lives prior to salvation and after salvation, as if it is one continuous life. Someone will say that it is foolishness to pretend that your life before salvation never existed, because clearly it did. If you were married before you were saved you are still married after you are saved. If you incurred debt before you were saved, then you still owe that debt after you are saved. People who make these comments, struggle to differentiate between the natural and the spiritual. In the natural, we do have one continuous life, but in the spirit, this is not the case. In the spirit, when we accept Jesus Christ as our Lord and Saviour, we become a complete new creation that never existed before. This truth is revealed to us in second Corinthians chapter five quoted above. So, what am I saying? I am not saying that because we are born-again that we can now walk away from our previous life in the natural, for scripture plainly tells us to remain in the same calling in which we are called. What I am saying is that one should not dwell in the past. Talk as little as possible about your life before you were saved (unless it forms part of your testimony when witnessing to others, that they may be saved) and do not think about it. Why dwell on that which God Himself, no longer acknowledges. On our day of judgement, believers will not be held to account for anything done before they were saved. No matter how sinful and wicked a life they may have led. Everything has been wiped out by nailing it to the cross, as revealed to us in Colossians chapter two above. But equally, believers will also not be rewarded for any supposedly good deed done before they were saved, for all those works would have been done in the flesh anyway, and not in the love of Christ.

## We are judged at the first resurrection

*Revelation 6:9-11 "When He opened the fifth seal, I saw under the altar the souls of those who had been slain for the word of God and for the testimony which they held. (10) And they cried with a loud voice, saying, "How long, O Lord, holy and true, until You judge and avenge our blood on those who dwell on the earth?" (11) Then a white robe was given to each of them; and it was said to them that they should rest a little while longer, until both the number of their fellow servants and their brethren, who would be killed as they were, was completed."*

*Revelation 14:13 "Then I heard a voice from heaven saying to me, "Write: 'Blessed are the dead who die in the Lord from now on.' " "Yes," says the Spirit, "that they may rest from their labours, and their works follow them."*

*Daniel 12:13 "But you, go your way till the end; for you shall rest, and will arise to your inheritance at the end of the days."*

It is important to note that those who fall asleep in Christ, do not stand before the judgment seat of Christ, when they go to be with the Lord. When we go to be with the Lord Jesus, it is to rest from our works. In the book of

# The saints' judgement

Revelations chapter six quoted above, the Holy Spirit reveals to us that all those who have been martyred for the Lord Jesus, are currently resting in heaven. They are told to continue resting, until the time that all of their number would have been completed. That number has not yet been completed, for there are many more of the Lord's saints that are still to be martyred for their faith in Him. The saints that are resting under the altar of God includes all the Lord's martyrs, beginning from Abel who was killed by his brother Cain over six thousand years ago. The Lord's martyrs are not working in heaven, they are resting. All the saints who have gone to be with the Lord in heaven, are resting from their works, for their time for works has ended. In Revelation chapter fourteen quoted above, the Holy Spirit clearly teaches us that all who die in the Lord Jesus, go to Him to rest from their labours and that their works follow them. When one rests from their labours, it means exactly that. There are no saints working in heaven today. The Holy Spirit cannot make it any plainer than that. The reason that our works follow us to heaven, is because people follow us to heaven. The works that we do while on the earth, is to build into the lives of others. When we go to be with the Lord, those whom we have ministered to while on the earth, will eventually follow us to be with Him. In Daniel chapter twelve quoted above, the Holy Spirit again reveals to us that the saints rest when they fall asleep. In this passage of scripture, the angel Gabriel told Daniel that when he came to the end of his time on the earth, that he would enter into his rest and that he would rise at the end of the days. The end of the days when Daniel will rise, is at the resurrection of all the saints, at our Lord's second coming. Gabriel also told Daniel that he will only receive his inheritance, at that resurrection. The reason that Daniel will only receive his inheritance at the first resurrection, is because it is only then that the saints' works will be judged. And it is only as a result of our works being judged, that we will receive our rewards from the Lord.

*Colossians 4:12 "Epaphras, who is one of you, a bondservant of Christ, greets you, always labouring fervently for you in prayers, that you may stand perfect and complete in all the will of God."*

*Galatians 4:19 "My little children, for whom I labour in birth again until Christ is formed in you."*

As believers, we labour here on the earth. Part of our labours that we perform while on the earth, is prayer. In Colossians chapter four quoted above, the apostle Paul teaches us that he and his ministry team laboured fervently in prayers for the saints. When Paul stated, as quoted from Galatians chapter four above, that he laboured in birth again until Christ was formed in the churches in Galatia, he was referring to the prayers and supplications that he offered to God on their behalf. Over the centuries and even currently, there have been fables and false visions spread in the church, that the saints in heaven are praying for the saints on the earth. The reason that Satan has tried to bring this lie into the church, is to try and lure them to then pray to the saints in heaven, to ask them to intercede on their behalf. Such prayers are futile, for no one hears them. Our Lord Jesus has taught His church to pray to the Father, by the Spirit, in the name of Jesus. We have seen earlier, that the scripture says that our works follow us. The works that we do on earth account to us as fruit for eternity. There are many saints in heaven today who are still reaping fruit for eternity, based on their works that are still blessing the body of Christ on the earth today. You say how is that possible? The bible is full of accounts of saints who, through their testimonies and teachings, have built with silver, gold and precious stones into the lives of myriads of believers over the centuries, and are still doing so today. And then there are the saints who have left writings behind, outside of the bible, which have also blessed and continue to bless the body of Christ today. Not to mention all the other media avenues available to the body of Christ today, from saints that have since gone to be with the Lord Jesus. Heavens books are not yet closed, and the final tally has not yet been made, and no saint has yet received any reward from our Lord and Master. There is a set day in the future when all the works of all Christians, will be judged.

*Revelation 11:15-18 "Then the seventh angel sounded: And there were loud voices in heaven, saying, "The kingdoms of this world have become the kingdoms of our Lord and of His Christ, and He shall reign forever and ever!" ... (18) The nations were angry, and Your wrath has come, And the time of the dead, that they should be judged, and that You should reward Your servants the prophets and the saints, and those who fear Your name, small and great, and should destroy those who destroy the earth."*

*Psalms 50:1-6 "The Mighty One, God the LORD, has spoken and called the earth from the rising of the sun to its going down. ... (4) He shall call to the heavens from above, and to the earth, that He may judge His people: (5) "Gather My saints together to Me, those who have made a covenant with Me by sacrifice." (6) Let the heavens declare His righteousness, For God Himself is Judge."*

*Luke 14:14 "And you will be blessed, because they cannot repay you; for you shall be repaid at the resurrection of the just."*

*1 Corinthians 4:5 "Therefore judge nothing before the time, until the Lord comes, who will both bring to light the hidden things of darkness and reveal the counsels of the hearts. Then each one's praise will come from God."*

Scripture plainly reveals to us, that the Lord's saints will be judged by Him at His second coming, when the first resurrection takes place. And it is only when we are judged, that we will receive our rewards from the Lord Jesus. Until that time, no saints will be judged, and consequently no saints have yet received or can receive any rewards, which includes all thrones that will be given by Him. In Revelations chapter eleven quoted above, we see that the saints will be judged and rewarded, at the time that the seventh trumpet shall sound. The seventh angel will only sound his trumpet at the end of the age. None of the Lord's saints will be judged or rewarded, before that time. In Psalms chapter fifty quoted above, again the Holy Spirit has spoken clearly to let us know that our Lord Jesus will judge His saints, when He returns to the earth to reign upon the earth. For our Lord says that His angels will gather His saints to Him when He returns to the earth, so that He may judge His people. And he tells us that His saints will be gathered from both heaven and the earth. Our Lord is clearly referring to the first resurrection in this passage of scripture. We saw earlier in second Timothy chapter four, that even though Paul was assured that he would receive the crown of righteousness as his reward from the Lord, Paul knew that he would not receive it when he went to be with the Lord. He would only receive that crown on the appointed day, when all Christians would receive their rewards according to their works done on the earth. In Luke chapter fourteen quoted above, our Lord Jesus has plainly told us that we will only be rewarded for our works at the time of the first resurrection, and not before. In Matthew chapter nineteen, our Lord Jesus also plainly said to the disciples, that thrones will only be given to His saints at the time of the regeneration, referring to the time of the first resurrection (for more detail on this point see my book "Resurrection of the Dead"). That time has not yet come. In one Corinthians chapter four quoted above, the Holy Spirit reveals to us that our Lord Jesus will only judge His church when He returns to the earth, not before. For He counsels us through the apostle Paul, to judge nothing before the time, until the Lord comes. And so, we see that scripture is very clear that there is a set day in the future, when all the Lord's saints will be judged by Him at the same time. That set day will occur at His second coming, which is when the resurrection of the saints will occur. It is only on that day of judgement that the saints will be rewarded for their works, which will include any thrones that may be given to His saints. Until that day, scripture again plainly teaches us that all saints who fall asleep, go to rest in the presence of the Lord. And so just as there have been false visions spread in the church that the saints in heaven are praying for the saints on earth, there have also been false visions spread in the church, of saints who have already received their thrones from God. None of this is true. For thrones, will only be given on that set day.

# The saints' judgement

# Chapter 3
# Our works will be judged
## Everything will be judged

*Matthew 16:27 "For the Son of Man will come in the glory of His Father with His angels, and then He will reward each according to his works."*

*2 Corinthians 5:9-10 "Therefore we make it our aim, whether present or absent, to be well pleasing to Him. (10) For we must all appear before the judgment seat of Christ, that each one may receive the things done in the body, according to what he has done, whether good or bad."*

*Romans 2:14-16 "for when Gentiles, who do not have the law, by nature do the things in the law, these, although not having the law, are a law to themselves, (15) who show the work of the law written in their hearts, their conscience also bearing witness, and between themselves their thoughts accusing or else excusing them (16) in the day when God will judge the secrets of men by Jesus Christ, according to my gospel."*

In the book of Revelation when our Lord Jesus spoke to each of the seven churches in Asia, He opened each of His addresses to those churches with the following statement, "I know your works". Jesus still says those exact same words to every church on the earth today. And He also says those same words to every individual believer on the earth today. Jesus watches our works. He watches our works because as believers, it is our works that will be judged by Him on that day. In Matthew chapter sixteen quoted above, our Lord plainly tells us that He will reward us according to the works that we have done. Every saint will stand before the Lord Jesus on that day, to give an account to Him for their time on the earth. The works that will be judged, will be those works we have done from the time we are born again, until the time that we leave our earthly tents to be with the Lord. As believers, we will be judged by our Lord Jesus on that day, for all that we have done in the body, both good and bad. Most Christians think that only their good works will be judged on that day. But as quoted in two Corinthians chapter five above, the Holy Spirit through the apostle Paul, tells us plainly that every work we have done will be judged, both good and bad. As we examine our works that will be judged on that day, we need to clarify that under the category of works everything is included, every thought, every word spoken and every deed done. It is extremely important for us to realise that everything will be judged. Nothing will be left out. Heaven's records are absolute, and cover every thought, every word spoken and every deed done, during our time here on earth. In Romans chapter two quoted above, the Holy Spirit reveals to us through the apostle Paul, that the secrets of men's hearts will be judged on that day. Those thoughts that you may have thought no one knew about have all been recorded in heaven, and we will have to give an account for each one. Those thoughts that were pleasing to God will be praised on that day, while those thoughts that were not pleasing to Him, will cause us to be ashamed on that day.

# Our works will be judged

*1 Corinthians 4:3-5 "But with me it is a very small thing that I should be judged by you or by a human court. In fact, I do not even judge myself. (4) For I know of nothing against myself, yet I am not justified by this; but He who judges me is the Lord. (5) Therefore, judge nothing before the time, until the Lord comes, who will both bring to light the hidden things of darkness and reveal the counsels of the hearts. Then each one's praise will come from God."*

*Matthew 12:36-37 "But I say to you that for every idle word men may speak; they will give account of it in the day of judgment. (37) For by your words you will be justified, and by your words you will be condemned."*

*Hebrews 6:10 "For God is not unjust to forget your work and labor of love which you have shown toward His name, in that you have ministered to the saints, and do minister."*

In the passage of scripture from one Corinthians chapter four quoted above, the Holy Spirit through the apostle Paul, reveals to us plainly that God will reveal the thoughts of our hearts, on that day. Nothing will be hidden on that day. Everything will be brought into the light, and everything will be brought to account. The scripture tells us that love thinks no evil. Do your thoughts line up with our Lord's commandment to walk in love? In Matthew chapter twelve quoted above, our Lord Jesus said that we will have to give an account for every idle word spoken on that day. So, what are our idle words?

These are the words we speak in our everyday conversations that we have with believers and nonbelievers alike. Think about that. Do the words that you speak in your daily conversations, meet God's requirement that no corrupt word is to proceed out of your mouth, but what is good for necessary edification, that it may impart grace to the hearers? Our words spoken will either receive praise from our Lord Jesus on that day, or cause us to be ashamed before Him on that day. It is important to note that no good work that we have done, will be forgotten on that day. From the time that we are born-again, every good work we do is recorded in heaven and cannot be blotted out. In Hebrews chapter six quoted above, the Holy Spirit tells us that God is not unjust. And because He is not unjust, He will not forget the good works that we have done while on the earth. Every good work done, will be rewarded on that day. There are some works done on the earth however, that can be blotted out. And these works will not be remembered on that day. The works that I am referring to are all sins that we commit, which we repent of and ask His forgiveness for. Our Lord is faithful and just to forgive us our sins, and they are blotted out of heavens records by His precious blood. You can readily see then why it is necessary that we keep a short account of sin, and confess them before the Lord as soon as they are committed. For sin that is unforgiven remains on heavens records, and will be brought to account on that day. For we will be held to account, for both the good and the bad that we have done. When you realise just how thorough our judgement will be, you will understand just why we need to walk in the fullness of grace provided to us, through Jesus Christ our Lord. Time and again the writers of the new testament admonish us, to walk worthy of the calling that we have received. Our day of judgement is not to be taken lightly, and we should approach it with the same purpose that Paul displayed.

## Works that will be rewarded

*Romans 8:4 "that the righteous requirement of the law might be fulfilled in us who do not walk according to the flesh but according to the spirit."*

*Matthew 5:17-19 "Do not think that I came to destroy the Law or the Prophets. I did not come to destroy but to fulfil. (18) For assuredly, I say to you, till heaven and earth pass away, one jot or one tittle will by no means pass from the law till all is fulfilled. (19) Whoever therefore breaks one of the least of these commandments, and teaches men so, shall be called least in the kingdom of heaven; but whoever does and teaches them, he shall be called great in the kingdom of heaven."*

So, what works will be rewarded by the Lord Jesus on that day? The answer to that question for the new covenant saint, is very simple. Under the new covenant, we are born-again, and it is our spirits that have become new creations in Christ Jesus. Because our spirits are born of God they are perfect, and they will always do that which pleases the Father. However, there is a part of man that does not change at the new birth. That part of man is called the flesh, and is made up of our physical bodies and the unrenewed mind. Just as our spirits will always do that which pleases God our Father, so the flesh will always be at enmity with God and His word. The reason for that is because sin dwells in our flesh. Although all believers have eternal life in their spirits, not all walk in the spirit. Many still walk in the flesh. Born-again believers at all times, are either walking in the spirit or they are walking in the flesh. There is no grey area. In Romans chapter eight quoted above, the Holy Spirit through the apostle Paul, counsels all believers to walk in the spirit and not in the flesh. For those who walk in the spirit, fulfil the righteous requirements of the law. In Matthew chapter five quoted above, our Lord Jesus gives us some insight as to just what will be rewarded on our day of judgement. He tells us that those who do the commandments of God and teaches others to do the same, will be called great in the kingdom of heaven. You will recall that our Lord Jesus has given His church a new commandment under the new covenant. And that commandment is that we should love one another, as He has loved us. For the saint that keeps this commandment and teaches others to do the same, they can expect to be called great in the kingdom of heaven on that day. In the flesh, it is impossible to keep this commandment. It is only by walking in the spirit, that the believer can keep the commandment of love. And we can only walk in the spirit by faith. And so consequently, all works done in the spirit will be rewarded on that day. The more we walk in the spirit in this life, the more we will be rewarded on that day.

*Colossians 3:23-24 "And whatever you do, do it heartily, as to the Lord and not to men, (24) knowing that from the Lord you will receive the reward of the inheritance; for you serve the Lord Christ."*

# Our works will be judged

*Ephesians 6:5-8 "Bondservants, be obedient to those who are your masters according to the flesh, with fear and trembling, in sincerity of heart, as to Christ; (6) not with eye service, as men-pleasers, but as bondservants of Christ, doing the will of God from the heart, (7) with goodwill doing service, as to the Lord, and not to men, (8) knowing that whatever good anyone does, he will receive the same from the Lord, whether he is a slave or free."*

*1 Corinthians 13:3 "And though I bestow all my goods to feed the poor, and though I give my body to be burned, but have not love, it profits me nothing."*

In Colossians chapter three quoted above, the word translated "heartily" is an unfortunate translation, because that word does not communicate clearly to us what the Holy Spirit is saying. A more accurate translation of the word "heartily", would be to say, "out of the spirit". And so, this verse of scripture should read, *"And whatever you do, do it out of the spirit, as to the Lord and not to men, knowing that from the Lord you will receive the reward of the inheritance; for you serve the Lord Christ."* Clearly from this passage of scripture, the Holy Spirit is teaching us that that which is done in the spirit, will be rewarded on that day. For it is the works that are done in the spirit that will endure, and not be burned up on that day. In Ephesians chapter six quoted above, the Holy Spirit through the apostle Paul, reinforces this truth when He writes to the church. For He tells them that doing the will of God from the heart, is what will be rewarded on that day. In other words, doing the will of God out of the spirit is what will be rewarded on that day. In one

# Our works will be judged

Corinthians chapter thirteen quoted above, the Holy Spirit reveals to us that even the most benevolent works done outside of the love of God, will count for nothing on the day of judgement. The reason for that, is because those works will have been done in the flesh. The flesh does good works to be recognised by men. The spirit does good works to please the Father. Two individuals can do exactly the same work, i.e. they can both bestow all their goods to feed the poor. From the outside, both works look exactly the same, and we would think that both will be rewarded equally by the Lord Jesus on that day. However, God looks on the heart, and only that work done from the spirit will be rewarded on that day, while the other will be burned up, as it was done in the flesh. We can only walk in the love of God by walking in the spirit.

*Matthew 10:42 "And whoever gives one of these little ones only a cup of cold water in the name of a disciple, assuredly, I say to you, he shall by no means lose his reward."*

*Matthew 26:6-13 "And when Jesus was in Bethany at the house of Simon the leper, (7) a woman came to Him having an alabaster flask of very costly fragrant oil, and she poured it on His head as He sat at the table. (8) But when His disciples saw it, they were indignant, saying, "Why this waste? (9) For this fragrant oil, might have been sold for much and given to the poor." (10) But when Jesus was aware of it, He said to them, "Why do you trouble the woman? For she has done a good work for Me. (11) For you have the poor with you always, but Me you do not have always. (12) For in pouring this*

# Our works will be judged

*fragrant oil on My body, she did it for My burial. (13) Assuredly, I say to you, wherever this gospel is preached in the whole world, what this woman has done will also be told as a memorial to her."*

Heavens account of our good works done, are far more detailed than we can begin to imagine. There will be works for which we will be rewarded on that day, that we never imagined heaven would have noticed, but nothing goes unrewarded in heaven. In Matthew chapter ten quoted above, our Lord Jesus stated that something that to us may seem trivial, such as giving someone a cup of cold water in the name of a disciple, would not go unrewarded on that day. When viewed in the natural, a work done in the spirit does not always look like a good work. Remember that the scriptures tell us that spiritual things are foolishness to the natural man. This is one of the reasons that the Holy Spirit through the apostle Paul, tells us to judge nothing before the time. For on that day God, will reveal the motives of the heart for the works that have been done in this life. Again, I must emphasize that God looks on the heart. In Matthew chapter twenty-six quoted above, the Holy Spirit records an example of a work done in the spirit that will be rewarded on that day. Mary was led by the Spirit of God to anoint the Lord Jesus with costly fragrant oil, in preparation for His burial that He was about to undergo. In the natural this was not a good work at all, because of the apparent waste of that money not being diverted to the more "noble" work of giving to the poor. And all who looked at what she did that night, condemned her for what they deemed extravagant waste. But in the spirit, this was an exceptional work that Mary did, and she will be rewarded by our Lord Jesus on that day, for that work. Scripture is very clear about the fact that all works done in the spirit will be rewarded on that day, while all works done in the flesh will be burned up and thus go unrewarded. If your desire is to be rewarded on your day of judgement, then I would encourage you to only walk in the spirit.

### Doing His works

*Romans 12:1-2 "I beseech you therefore, brethren, by the mercies of God, that you present your bodies a living sacrifice, holy, acceptable to God, which is your reasonable service.  (2)  And do not be conformed to this world, but be transformed by the renewing of your mind, that you may prove what is that good and acceptable and perfect will of God."*

*Ephesians 2:10 "For we are His workmanship, created in Christ Jesus for good works, which God prepared beforehand that we should walk in them."*

*1 Peter 4:10 "As each one has received a gift, minister it to one another, as good stewards of the manifold grace of God."*

*Ephesians 4:7-16 "But to each one of us grace was given according to the measure of Christ's gift. ... (16) from whom the whole body, joined and knit together by what every joint supplies, according to the effective working by which every part does its*

# Our works will be judged

*share, causes growth of the body for the edifying of itself in love."*

There is another aspect of our lives, that will be judged on that day. We will also be held to account for the works that we should have done, but which we failed to do. This aspect of judgment, pertains to God's perfect will for our lives. As a result of us failing to fulfil God's perfect will for our lives, we will lose those rewards that should have been ours. In Romans chapter twelve quoted above, the Holy Spirit through the apostle Paul, reveals to us that God has His permissible will (the word translated "acceptable" is also translated permissible), and He also has His perfect will. We are encouraged by the Holy Spirit in this passage of scripture to prove or find out, what God's perfect will is. In other words, we are encouraged to find out what God's perfect will is for our lives. God's permissible will, means exactly that. God will permit His children to live as they so choose (not sinfully obviously). I would estimate that for various reasons, most believers walk only in God's permissible will. But God also has His perfect will for our lives. In Ephesians chapter two quoted above, the Holy Spirit teaches us that we are God's workmanship. In other words, we are what we are, because God has made us that way. For example, some of us are artistic, while others are good administrators. Each of us have God given talents. Many have taken those talents, and used them for their own benefit and gain in this life. And there is nothing wrong with that, up to a point. But I want you to notice the rest of that verse of scripture. There is a primary reason that God has made us the way we are. That reason is so that we can accomplish the good works in Christ, that God has already prepared for us to walk in. There are specific works that only we as individuals can walk in, because they have been prepared for us by God. Those works relate to the gift that each one of us have received from the Lord. It is this gift which He expects us to minister to His body. In one Peter chapter four quoted above, the Holy Spirit through the apostle Peter, reinforces the truth that each one of the Lord's saints has received at least one gift from Him. And that our Lord expects us to minister that gift to one another, as good stewards of His manifested grace in our lives. It is up to the individual believer to seek the Lord to find out from Him what gifting they have received, and just how He wants them to minister their gift to His body. When we don't walk in those works, then the body of Christ is deprived of the blessing that God intended. In Ephesians chapter four quoted above, the Lord makes it very clear that when every part of the body does its share, then the body will grow as God intended. When believers do not walk in the works God has prepared for them, then they are not doing their share. And they will be held to account on that day for their disobedience. But at the same time, by failing to walk in those good works, they will also lose out on the rewards that have been laid up in heaven for them.

### Reward is also relative to cost

*Luke 21:1-4 "And He looked up and saw the rich putting their gifts into the treasury, (2) and He saw also a certain poor widow putting in two mites. (3) So, He said, "Truly I say to you that this poor widow has put in more than all; (4) for all these out of their abundance have put in offerings for God, but*

# Our works will be judged

*she out of her poverty put in all the livelihood that she had."*

*1 Corinthians 9:16-18 "For if I preach the gospel, I have nothing to boast of, for necessity is laid upon me; yes, woe is me if I do not preach the gospel! (17) For if I do this willingly, I have a reward; but if against my will, I have been entrusted with a stewardship. (18) What is my reward then? That when I preach the gospel, I may present the gospel of Christ without charge, that I may not abuse my authority in the gospel."*

It also needs to be said that heaven places a different value on our works. The value of our heavenly reward for our good works is never based on the impact or size of our good works, but is always based on the sacrifice that we have made in order to do those good works. In Luke's gospel chapter twenty-one quoted above, our Lord Jesus gave us a clear example of this principle. The poor widow gave the least of all, that day. But the cost she incurred to give that day, was far greater than all. Heaven never rewards us in proportion to the amount that we have given, it always rewards us in proportion to the cost that we have incurred in that giving. This poor widow will be rewarded in heaven immeasurably more, than all others that gave on that day. The others who gave on that day will also be rewarded, but their reward will not be comparable to hers. Let's look at another example. In one Corinthians chapter nine quoted above, the apostle Paul teaches us a very valuable lesson in relation to our rewards received for the specific works that our Lord Jesus has called each of us to perform on the earth. The

# Our works will be judged

principle that I want you to see here, is that even though Paul was preaching the gospel and impacting the lives of multitudes, he stated that he should not expect to be rewarded for doing this. In fact, he stated that he would incur woe if he did not preach the gospel. Why would Paul say something like that? He said it because he understood the principle of the proportion of heavens rewards being based on not only what good works we do, but also on the cost incurred by us in doing those good works. The simple act of preaching the gospel was not costing Paul very much, because he had received that ability (stewardship) from the Lord. The Lord had however, commanded that those who preach the gospel should live by the gospel. And so, Paul had decided that he would forgo this right and preach the gospel free of charge, i.e. not take up offerings for his ministry. In this way, it would cost Paul to preach the gospel, and so he could expect heaven's reward for doing that which God had instructed him and enabled him, to do.

*Matthew 19:27-29 "Then Peter answered and said to Him, "See, we have left all and followed You. Therefore, what shall we have?" (28) So, Jesus said to them, "Assuredly I say to you, that in the regeneration, when the Son of Man sits on the throne of His glory, you who have followed Me will also sit on twelve thrones, judging the twelve tribes of Israel. (29) And everyone who has left houses or brothers or sisters or father or mother or wife or children or lands, for My name's sake, shall receive a hundredfold, and inherit eternal life."*

# Our works will be judged

*Luke 17:7-10 "And which of you, having a servant ploughing or tending sheep, will say to him when he has come in from the field, 'Come at once and sit down to eat'? (8) But will he not rather say to him, 'Prepare something for my supper, and gird yourself and serve me till I have eaten and drunk, and afterward you will eat and drink'? (9) Does he thank that servant because he did the things that were commanded him? I think not. (10) So likewise you, when you have done all those things which you are commanded, say, 'We are unprofitable servants. We have done what was our duty to do.'"*

In Matthew's gospel quoted above, our Lord Jesus reinforces the principle of heavens rewards being directly related to the cost incurred by His disciples, in doing the works He called them to do. For Peter asks Him, what rewards the disciples can expect to receive, seeing that they had left all to follow Him. Our Lord answered, that they would be seated on thrones judging the twelve tribes of Israel. But our Lord did not stop there, for He went on to say, that everyone who left all and followed Him for the sake of the gospel, could expect to receive a one hundredfold reward of that which they had left behind, and eternal life. Not all believers are prepared to make this degree of sacrifice, and in fact not all believers are called to make this degree of sacrifice. However, for those who are called and obey, they can expect to receive the one hundredfold reward that our Lord Jesus spoke about. The principle is clear. Heaven's rewards for good works, are in direct relation to the cost incurred in doing those good works. In Luke chapter seventeen quoted above, our Lord Jesus reinforced the fact that doing God's will for our lives, in and of itself, is no guarantee of our being rewarded in heaven. For our Lord tells us that when we are obedient to do the works which our Lord calls us to do, that our attitude should be that we are just unprofitable servants who have done what we were commanded to do. So, is the Lord saying that those who are called to preach the gospel and are obedient to that call, cannot expect any reward from Him, on that day? No, He is not, because elsewhere in scripture we are taught that those who are faithful in their callings, will be rewarded on that day. The Lord Jesus is dealing with the principle of cost here, and so what He is saying is that the proportion of reward that they can expect is in relation to the cost that they have incurred in obeying that call. This principle applies to every good work that our Lord Jesus has called us to do.

### Great reward for suffering

*Philippians 1:29 "For to you it has been granted on behalf of Christ, not only to believe in Him, but also to suffer for His sake."*

*1 Peter 4:14-16 "If you are reproached for the name of Christ, blessed are you, for the Spirit of glory and of God rests upon you. On their part He is blasphemed, but on your part He is glorified. (15) But let none of you suffer as a murderer, a thief, an evildoer, or as a busybody in other people's matters. (16) Yet if anyone suffers as a Christian, let him not be ashamed, but let him glorify God in this matter."*

*Acts 5:40-41 "And they agreed with him, and when they had called for the apostles and beaten them, they commanded that they should not speak in the name of Jesus, and let them go. (41) So, they departed from the presence of the council, rejoicing that they were counted worthy to suffer shame for His name."*

There is one further good work that will be greatly rewarded on that day. And that good work is to suffer for the Lord Jesus and for His gospel. When I refer to suffering here, I am not referring to suffering the trials of life that everyone suffers from time to time. I am specifically referring to the suffering incurred by the believer, because of persecution for their belief in Jesus Christ and His gospel. Because heaven places tremendous value on this particular good work, God the Father decides who is counted worthy to suffer for our Lord Jesus and His gospel. Some will suffer more than others, purely because God has deemed them worthy to suffer more. In Philippians chapter one quoted above, we learn that the church at Philippi had received this blessing. Because the Holy Spirit through the apostle Paul, tells them that it had been granted to them to suffer for the sake of Christ. The believers in Philippi were experiencing the same persecutions that Paul and Silas had endured when they first preached the gospel in that city. You will recall that Paul and Silas were beaten with rods in that city, and then they had been thrown into prison. God miraculously delivered His two ministers on that occasion. But after Paul and Silas had left the city, persecution had broken out against the believers there, and many of them had been imprisoned for their faith in Christ. In one Peter chapter four quoted above, the apostle Peter encourages those who incur suffering in this life, because of their walk as believers. He tells us that those particular believers are blessed because the Spirit of glory rests upon them, and that they are not to be ashamed for suffering as Christians but rather that they should glorify God in this. The apostles of the Lamb had received first hand teaching from our Lord Jesus regarding the fact that those who suffer for the gospel can expect great reward in heaven, and because of this fact that not all believers will be counted worthy to suffer for the gospel. In the book of Acts chapter five quoted above, we see the account of when these apostles had received their first beating, because of their preaching of the gospel. Notice their absolute joy at having been counted worthy by the Father to suffer for the gospel of His Son, Jesus Christ our Lord.

*Matthew 5:10-12 "Blessed are those who are persecuted for righteousness' sake, for theirs is the kingdom of heaven. (11) "Blessed are you when they revile and persecute you, and say all kinds of evil against you falsely for My sake. (12) Rejoice and be exceedingly glad, for great is your reward in heaven, for so they persecuted the prophets who were before you."*

*Revelation 6:9-11 "When He opened the fifth seal, I saw under the altar the souls of those who had been slain for the word of God and for the testimony which they held. (10) And they cried with a loud voice, saying, "How long, O Lord, holy and true, until You judge and avenge our blood on those who dwell on the earth?" (11) Then a white robe was given to each of them; and it was said to them that*

# Our works will be judged



*they should rest a little while longer, until both the
number of their fellow servants and their brethren,
who would be killed as they were, was completed."*

In Matthew's gospel chapter five quoted above, our
Lord Jesus plainly teaches us that there is great reward in
heaven, for those who suffer persecution for their belief in
Him and His gospel. Many will be persecuted purely
because of their walk as Christians, in the midst of a
wicked society. Many will also be persecuted for their
proclaiming of the gospel of Jesus Christ. Let me say that
believers are not instructed in scripture, to seek out this
sort of persecution. Our Lord plainly taught us not to cast
our pearls before swine, lest they trample them underfoot,
turn on you and tear you. We need to be discerning as to
where and when our Lord wants us to preach His gospel.
I'm not talking about our walk as believers, for we live our
lives as Christians wherever we find ourselves. We are to
be living epistles, known and read by all men. I am talking
specifically about the preaching of the gospel. Let me
illustrate by means of an example. Paul and his ministry
team had been seeking God's guidance as to where He
wanted them to preach the gospel. There were two specific
areas where they wanted to preach, but the Holy Spirit
forbade them. The areas in question, were Asia and
Bithynia. God then told them to go to Macedonia to
preach there, and they went to the city of Philippi in
obedience to God's perfect will. When they got there, God
opened the door for them to add numerous souls to the
kingdom. But as we read earlier, it was also in this city
that Paul and Silas were beaten and thrown in prison for
obediently preaching the gospel. This sort of persecution
will come your way if God allows it, even when you are in

# Our works will be judged

His perfect will. I have no doubt that had Paul and his team gone into Asia and Bithynia to preach, they would have experienced similar or even worse persecution, with no converts. We are not to seek this type of persecution. It will come to those whom God deems worthy. And then we come to the saints who are counted worthy of our Lord Jesus, to be one of His faithful martyrs. In the book of Revelation chapter six quoted above, we have clear evidence of just how much value God the Father places on the death of our Lord's martyrs. This is displayed in the fact that they are separated in heaven, from the rest of His saints. Each one of them are currently resting under the altar of the Almighty God. Their reward on that day, will be great indeed, and deservedly so.

## Works done in the flesh

*1 Corinthians 3:8-15 "Now he who plants and he who waters are one, and each one will receive his own reward according to his own labour. (9) For we are God's fellow workers; you are God's field; you are God's building. (10) According to the grace of God which was given to me, as a wise master builder I have laid the foundation, and another builds on it. But let each one take heed how he builds on it. (11) For no other foundation can anyone lay than that which is laid, which is Jesus Christ. (12) Now if anyone builds on this foundation with gold, silver, precious stones, wood, hay, straw, (13) each one's work will become clear; for the Day will declare it, because it will be revealed by fire; and the fire will test each one's work, of what sort it is. (14) If anyone's work which he has built on it endures, he will receive a reward. (15) If anyone's work is burned, he will suffer loss; but he himself will be saved, yet so as through fire."*

We saw earlier that under the new covenant the born-again believer, at all times, is either walking in the spirit or they are walking in the flesh. As we have seen that all works done in the spirit will be rewarded on that day, the exact opposite is true for all works done in the flesh. All works done in the flesh will be burned up on that day. If you have any desire to receive your eternal rewards from our Lord Jesus on that day, then I urge you to stay away from works done in the flesh. For all works done in the flesh will not survive the test of fire, and those saints will suffer loss on that day. Notice that I am not talking about the "works of the flesh" as listed in Galatians chapter five, but I am talking about "works done in the flesh". For there is a difference between the two. The "works of the flesh", is what scripture also calls sin. These works will be judged differently on that day. But there is such a thing as "works done in the flesh". These works are seemingly good works, and not sinful, and yet they are done in the flesh and not in the spirit. We see in one Corinthians chapter three quoted above, that it is possible that there are works that will be burned up on that day. For the saint whose works are burned up on that day, they will incur loss for eternity. So, let us relook at that scripture so that we can have a clearer understanding of just what those works are. In context, when the Holy Spirit reveals this truth to us, He is not talking about sin. For Paul's example, is of a minister who is labouring through the preaching of the gospel. And Paul is saying that it is possible that what this minister is teaching the church is not gold, silver and precious stones, but rather wood, hay and straw. So, what on the outside, seemingly looks like good works, will have the end result of not being sanctioned by heaven, and thus be burned up when those works are tried by fire. The key to not having your works burned up on that day, lies in verse nine of the scripture we have just looked at, *"For we are God's fellow workers"*. In that light let us now use the example given to us by the Holy Spirit, and re-examine the minister who built with wood, hay and straw. Had this minister preached the gospel as a fellow worker with the Holy Spirit, then the Holy Spirit would never have sanctioned him preaching with wood, hay and straw. But what happened is that this minister was preaching his own version of the gospel. He was not being led by the Holy Spirit in what he was preaching. He hadn't studied the word of God for himself, so that he could rightly divide the word of truth. Which is something that the Holy Spirit counsels all ministers of the gospel to do.

*2 Timothy 2:15 "Study to shew thyself approved unto God, a workman that needeth not to be ashamed, rightly dividing the word of truth."*

*Mark 7:6-9 "He answered and said to them, "Well did Isaiah prophesy of you hypocrites, as it is written: 'this people honours Me with their lips, but their heart is far from Me. (7) and in vain they worship Me, teaching as doctrines the commandments of men.' (8) For laying aside the commandment of God, you hold the tradition of men-- the washing of pitchers and cups, and many other such things you do." (9) He said to them, "All too well you reject the commandment of God, that you may keep your tradition."*

*Philippians 1:15-18 "Some indeed preach Christ even from envy and strife, and some also from goodwill: (16) The former preach Christ from selfish ambition, not sincerely, supposing to add affliction to my chains; (17) but the latter out of love, knowing that I am appointed for the defense of the gospel. (18) What then? Only that in every way, whether in pretence or in truth, Christ is preached; and in this I rejoice, yes, and will rejoice."*

Notice in second Timothy chapter two quoted above, that Paul teaches Timothy that the minister who does not rightly divide the word of truth, will eventually be ashamed. That minister will be ashamed before the Lord Jesus when our Lord reveals to him on that day, that what he taught was not what the bible taught. A wise minister of the gospel once said that he taught what he knew. If he found a verse of scripture that he did not understand, then he left that scripture alone until God showed him what it meant. The minister in the example in the letter to the Corinthians, had most probably gone to bible seminary and learnt what other men had taught him, which by and large were the traditions of men, and not the bible. Our Lord Jesus, in Mark chapter seven quoted above, exposes the problem that had arisen in Israel in His day. In that man's traditions were being taught as doctrine, and God's word was no longer taught as doctrine. You say but that was the Jews, not the church. Believe me, there are many traditions of men taught in the church today, that reject the word of God and make the word of God of no effect.

All of those traditions taught, and all error taught, will be burned up on that day. These ministers will be saved, but their works will be burned up. And then we come to the preaching of the gospel, which is done in the flesh. You say how is it possible to preach the gospel in the flesh? Any preaching that is pleasing to the flesh and accommodates the flesh, is not of God. You will find in certain churches and ministries, that only certain truths in the bible are taught, and those truths are taught to the extreme. Those ministers who preach in that manner are not being led by the Holy Spirit, they are preaching in the flesh to accommodate the flesh of baby believers. Mainly they are driven by covetousness. All of those works will be burned up on that day for they have been done in the flesh. In Philippians chapter one quoted above, the Holy Spirit reveals to us through the apostle Paul, that there are ministers of the gospel who preach the gospel from selfish ambition and not sincerely. There is an important point that we need to understand from this scripture. Those who receive the gospel that is preached, even from insincere ministers, will be blessed. But the minister who preaches insincerely, i.e. in the flesh, will not be rewarded by the Lord Jesus on that day. Even though the ones to whom they preached, were blessed through their preaching, for it is still Christ that is preached. We will look at the judgement of ministers of the gospel in another chapter, because their judgment will be different. Scripture clearly reveals to us that someone who preaches the gospel in the flesh and not in the spirit, will have their works burned up on that day.

*Matthew 6:1-4 "Take heed that you do not do your charitable deeds before men, to be seen by them. Otherwise you have no reward from your Father in heaven. (2) Therefore, when you do a charitable deed, do not sound a trumpet before you as the hypocrites do in the synagogues and in the streets, that they may have glory from men. Assuredly, I say to you, they have their reward. (3) But when you do a charitable deed, do not let your left hand know what your right hand is doing, (4) that your charitable deed may be in secret; and your Father who sees in secret will Himself reward you openly."*

*Colossians 3:22-24 "Bondservants, obey in all things your masters according to the flesh, not with eye service, as men-pleasers, but in sincerity of heart, fearing God. (23) And whatever you do, do it heartily, as to the Lord and not to men, (24) knowing that from the Lord you will receive the reward of the inheritance; for you serve the Lord Christ."*

So, what about those who do not preach the gospel? What about ordinary believers in the church? How will their works be judged as to what was done in the flesh, and what was done in the spirit? For all good works done in the spirit will be rewarded, but all seemingly good works done in the flesh will be burned up. Remember that in this section we are talking about seemingly good works, and not sinful works. In what is commonly referred to as our Lord's sermon on the mount, Jesus gave us numerous examples of works done in the flesh that will be burned up on that day. All of the works mentioned by our Lord Jesus in His teaching, were in and of themselves, good works. And so, on the outside when we see those good works, we think that the Lord will most certainly reward them. But our Lord does not look on the outside, our Lord looks on the heart. What the Lord Jesus taught us on that day was not rocket science. God will judge our motives. The works done in the spirit are those works in which our motive is to please God, as we are led by the Spirit of God, and not men. But the works done in the flesh are those works which are done to please men, and to receive recognition from men. In the example quoted from Matthew chapter six above, our Lord shows us how the same good work, such as doing a charitable deed, can be done in the flesh and also be done in the spirit. The good work done in the flesh is done to be recognized by men, and that work will be burned up on that day. The exact same good work done in the spirit, is done not to be recognized by men but to please the Father, and that work will be rewarded on that day. This principle can be applied to every area of your life. Every good work that you do in the spirit will be rewarded on that day. Every good work that you do in the flesh, will be burned up on that day. Then there are also just the normal daily lives of every believer. You will find two believers standing before the Lord Jesus on that day, who were both employed by the same company and did the same type of work. The one will be rewarded for their work done, and the other will have all that time at work burned up, resulting in their eternal loss. Why? The one did their everyday work as unto the Lord, i.e. they did even their everyday work in the spirit, and will thus be rewarded. The other worked for themselves and the progress of their own earthly careers, not working as unto the Lord, but rather trying to please their boss so that they could be promoted. All of their work was done in the flesh, and will be burned up on that day. Notice in Colossians chapter three quoted above, that the scripture says, "whatever you do". This principle applies to every area of our lives. Let me give you a bit of spiritual counsel here. The first thing you should do every morning when you open your eyes, even before you get out of bed, is commit to the Lord all that you will do that day as unto Him. You will find the Holy Spirit working in you throughout the day reminding you to do all as unto the Lord Jesus. You will find your day taking on a whole new perspective of wanting to please your Lord in all that you do. And you will be rewarded on that day.

## Some will incur a stricter judgement

*James 3:1 "My brethren, let not many of you become teachers, knowing that we shall receive a stricter judgment."*

*1 Timothy 1:5-7 "Now the purpose of the commandment is love from a pure heart, from a good conscience, and from sincere faith, (6) from which some, having strayed, have turned aside to idle talk, (7) desiring to be teachers of the law, understanding neither what they say nor the things which they affirm."*

The Lord, as the good Shepherd of the sheep, is very protective over His sheep. And He does not take kindly to any who would feed His sheep with anything that would cause them to stumble. In James chapter three quoted above, the Holy Spirit through the apostle James, counsels' believers not to be eager to become teachers in the church. When He makes this statement, He is not referring to those who are called and have received the ministry gift of teacher, for they have no choice in the matter. He is referring to ordinary believers, who have a desire to teach the bible. When any believer begins to teach fellow believers, they are no longer accountable to the Lord for their own actions only, but they have also become accountable to the Lord for the actions of others as well. For invariably, it is baby believers that are taught by other believers. There are two main areas where the believer who teaches others, will be held to account on that day. Firstly, that believer will be held to account for the example that they have set before the Lord's flock. For when baby believers listen to fellow believers teaching them the word of God, they also look at the lifestyles of those believers as examples of the way they should behave in the kingdom. You may be teaching the word correctly, but your lifestyle may be contrary to the word that you teach. Baby believers not only listen to what you teach, but they also then look at your lifestyle as a model for them to follow. If the way you live causes baby believers to stumble in their walk with the Lord, then you can readily see that it will not go very well with you on your day of judgement. Secondly, the believer who teaches others, will be held to account for what they teach. In one Timothy chapter one quoted above, the Holy Spirit through the apostle Paul, tells us of believers who were desiring to teach the law. The problem was that they didn't have a clue what they were teaching. They thought they did. But as it turns out they were teaching what amounted to idle talk and fables. Again, when baby believers hear this type of teaching they are affected, for they don't know any better. If what you teach causes baby believers to stumble in their walk with the Lord, then it will also not go well with you on your day of judgement. The Lord is not unjust to hold you to a greater degree of account on that day, because He didn't ask you to teach His sheep. You chose to do that of your own accord. There are many in the church who are desirous to teach the word of God, but few think of the eternal ramifications of their actions. Rather leave the teaching of God's word, to those whom He called and has enabled. This is not to say that fellow believers should never teach the word of God. Because scripture clearly teaches us that elders are chosen by the ministry gifts to shepherd the local church, and part of that shepherding is to teach. But in those instances, the ministry gifts first test potential elders to make sure they meet the requirements as laid down in scripture. And only those who qualify, are then placed into the position of elder in the church. These would be able to teach the word of God with confidence, and will be able to stand up to the stricter judgement they will incur on that day.

# Our works will be judged

# Chapter 4

# Unforgiven sin will be judged

## Judgement will be without partiality

*1 Timothy 5:19-25 "Do not receive an accusation against an elder except from two or three witnesses. (20) Those who are sinning rebuke in the presence of all, that the rest also may fear. ... (24) Some men's sins are clearly evident, preceding them to judgment, but those of some men follow later. (25) Likewise, the good works of some are clearly evident, and those that are otherwise cannot be hidden."*

*Matthew 5:18-19 "For assuredly, I say to you, till heaven and earth pass away, one jot or one tittle will by no means pass from the law till all is fulfilled. (19) Whoever therefore breaks one of the least of these commandments, and teaches men so, shall be called least in the kingdom of heaven; but whoever does and teaches them, he shall be called great in the kingdom of heaven."*

*1 Corinthians 4:3-5 "But with me it is a very small thing that I should be judged by you or by a human court. In fact, I do not even judge myself. (4) For I know of nothing against myself, yet I am not justified by this; but He who judges me is the Lord. (5) Therefore, judge nothing before the time, until the Lord comes, who will both bring to light the hidden things of darkness and reveal the counsels of the hearts. Then each one's praise will come from God."*

Now we come to an even more serious aspect of the believer's judgement, and that is unforgiven sin. In first Timothy chapter five quoted above, the Holy Spirit through the apostle Paul, reveals to us two aspects of our lives that we will be held to account for, on our day of judgement. Our good works, and also our sins. You will notice that when Paul makes the comment about some men's sins preceding them to judgement, that he was dealing with the issue of elders in the church who were sinning. Clearly this statement is made in relation to the judgement of believers, and not unbelievers. Then we also have the statement made by our Lord Jesus regarding believers who commit sin. In Matthew chapter five quoted above, our Lord Jesus is referring to believers. We know He is referring to believers, because He tells us that these individuals are in the kingdom of heaven. We also know that He is talking about believers who sin, because He speaks of those who break the commandments of God. And we know that to break God's commandments is to commit sin. Clearly, we see from this teaching that our Lord has given us, that sin in the life of the believer, will have an impact on their eternal standing in the kingdom of heaven. The reason for this, is because their sin will be brought to account on the day of judgement. In one Corinthians chapter four quoted above, the apostle Paul speaks of things that the Lord may have against him on that day. The only things that the Lord will have against His saints on that day, is unforgiven sin. Paul goes on to say that he was unaware that there was anything that the

# Unforgiven sin will be judged

Lord could hold against him. The reason Paul could say that, was because he made sure that he walked a blameless life before the Lord. Paul said of himself, that he always lived in all good conscience before God. How many believers do you know that can confidently say before the Lord, that they know of nothing against themselves? Paul did, and he told us to imitate him even as he imitated Christ. How many believers do you know that can confidently tell the church to imitate themselves as they imitate Christ? Again, Paul did. Someone said, but I thought that Paul said he was the chief of sinners. Paul did say that he was chief of sinners, before he was saved. The word translated "am" in that portion of scripture also means "was", which is the correct translation in the context of what Paul was teaching on.

*Colossians 3:23-25 "And whatever you do, do it heartily, as to the Lord and not to men, (24) knowing that from the Lord you will receive the reward of the inheritance; for you serve the Lord Christ. (25) But he who does wrong will be repaid for what he has done, and there is no partiality."*

*1 Peter 4:17-18 "For the time has come for judgment to begin at the house of God; and if it begins with us first, what will be the end of those who do not obey the gospel of God? (18) Now "if the righteous one is scarcely saved, where will the ungodly and the sinner appear?"*

*James 2:12-13 "So speak and so do as those who will be judged by the law of liberty. (13) For judgment is without mercy to the one who has shown no mercy. Mercy triumphs over judgment."*

In Colossians chapter three quoted above, the Holy Spirit through the apostle Paul, teaches us that the saints can expect to receive their reward from the Lord Jesus on that day, for those works that they have done in the spirit. But He also warns us that those saints who have done wrong, can also expect to receive their retribution from the Lord (the word translated "wrong" in this passage of scripture, can also be translated "sin"). The Holy Spirit emphasizes the point, by telling us that the Lord will not show partiality to those who have broken God's laws, just because they are His children. Make no mistake child of God, the believer's judgement will be thorough. The Lord will not overlook unforgiven sin. In one Peter chapter four quoted above, the Holy Spirit through the apostle Peter, teaches us that many believers will barely make it into heaven. For He says, pertaining to the saints' judgement, that the righteous one is scarcely saved. Unforgiven sin is not to be taken lightly. In James chapter two quoted above, the Holy Spirit through James the apostle, teaches us that we as believers, will be judged by the law of liberty on that day. In other words, we will be held to account according to God's laws under the new covenant, and whether we upheld them or not. When the Holy Spirit tells us that we will be judged by God's word, He then links mercy with that judgement. Only those who are found guilty, require mercy. So clearly there will be believers who will be found guilty of breaking God's laws on that day, and they will need to receive mercy from the Lord. In James's teaching, he tells us that one who has shown mercy to others during his life, can expect to receive mercy on that day, even though they may be found guilty. However, he tells us that those who have not shown mercy in this life, cannot expect mercy when they are judged on that day. The mercy referred to in this passage of scripture, pertains only to the judgement of the saints. For the unbelievers, will not experience mercy when they are raised to their judgement of condemnation.

*2 Timothy 1:16-18 "The Lord grant mercy to the household of Onesiphorus, for he often refreshed me, and was not ashamed of my chain; (17) but when he arrived in Rome, he sought me out very zealously and found me. (18) The Lord grant to him that he may find mercy from the Lord in that Day-and you know very well how many ways he ministered to me at Ephesus."*

*1 John 2:28-29 "And now, little children, abide in Him, that when He appears, we may have confidence and not be ashamed before Him at His coming. (29) If you know that He is righteous, you know that everyone who practices righteousness is born of Him."*

In two Timothy chapter one quoted above, the Holy Spirit through the apostle Paul, again gives us some insight as to just how strict the saint's judgement will be, on that day. The apostle Paul is speaking to Timothy about a fellow believer named Onesiphorus. Paul mentions this believer as one who has ministered to him in many ways. You would think that with a recommendation like that from one of the Lord's leading apostles, that he could expect to approach his day of judgement before the Lord

# Unforgiven sin will be judged

Jesus with great boldness. But note the comment made by Paul, specifically regarding his day of judgement. Paul prays that Onesiphorus may find mercy from the Lord Jesus on that day. Clearly
Onesiphorus will need mercy on that day, otherwise Paul would not have requested that the Lord grant him mercy on that day. James says that we all stumble in many things, so clearly, we will all need mercy from our Lord Jesus on that day. However, there will be believers who will stand before the Lord Jesus on that day, unashamed. In one John chapter two quoted above, the Holy Spirit said there would be. Those believers who have been abiding in Him, will have confidence before the Lord Jesus on that day, and will not be ashamed. The key is to abide in the Lord Jesus daily in this life, if you want to stand before the Lord Jesus unashamed on that day. In the very next verse of scripture, the Holy Spirit gives us some insight as to what it means to abide in the Lord Jesus. He tells us that the one who practices righteousness, qualifies. To practice righteousness means to stay away from sin. It is one thing to be made the righteousness of God in Christ Jesus, which every believer has become. But it is entirely a different thing, to practice the righteousness that we have become. Those believers who have not been practicing righteousness and have been continuing in sin, will not have confidence and will be ashamed before Him at His coming.

## Confessed sin will not be judged

# Unforgiven sin will be judged

*1 John 1:9 "If we confess our sins, He is faithful and just to forgive us our sins and to cleanse us from all unrighteousness."*

*Hebrews 10:17 "then He adds, "their sins and their lawless deeds I will remember no more." Matthew 6:11-12 "Give us this day our daily bread. (12) And forgive us our debts, as we forgive our debtors."*

Having said in the previous section, that we need to be practicing righteousness, brings us to the next point. Which is that as believers, there is one area of our lives that will not be judged. That area is all confessed sin, for which we have received forgiveness while we have been residing on the earth. In one John chapter one quoted above, the Holy Spirit through the apostle John, instructs us to confess our sins before the Lord. Obviously when we confess our sins, we are at the same time to repent of those sins and ask His forgiveness. The Holy Spirit tells us that if we do this, that our Lord Jesus is then faithful and just to forgive us our sins. All of those sins would have then been blotted out of heavens records by the blood of the Lamb, and will not be remembered on that day. There is a false teaching that has arisen in some parts of the church recently, that states that God has already forgiven every sin the believer commits, past, present and future. And so, they do not have to ask forgiveness for any sins they may commit. These believers are in for a shock on their day of judgement. When God forgives our sins, He remembers them no more. This truth is revealed to us in Hebrews chapter ten quoted above. And so, that which is forgiven in this age will not be brought to account in the age to come. Please note that I am talking about known sin that believers commit, not unknown sin committed in ignorance, or unintentional sin. For we can only confess known sin before the Lord. All sin committed in ignorance, and all unintentional sin, is cleansed immediately by the blood of the Lamb the moment that sin is committed, and will also not be remembered on that day (for more detail regarding this point see my book "Born Free from Sin"). Let me just expand on the point regarding known sin a little bit, because it is extremely important. Believers should keep a short account of their lives before the Lord at all times. What do I mean? In Matthew chapter six quoted above, when our Lord Jesus taught us on prayer, He taught us to ask our heavenly Father each day for our daily bread. Thus implying, that we should be praying at least once a day. In the very next verse of scripture, our Lord then taught us to ask our heavenly Father to forgive us our sins as we forgive others. And so, the principle is, that we should be confessing our sins and asking forgiveness for those sins, at least daily. Those who choose not to confess their sins daily, run the risk of forgetting past sins committed and thus not asking for those sins to be forgiven. Those sins which have not been forgiven, remain. And those sins will have to be accounted for on that day. I have seen believers swear at fellow believers in anger and then walk off, and I have wondered to myself if they would later repent before the Lord of their sin and ask His forgiveness or if they would just forget about it. Because if they did just forget about it, heaven certainly wouldn't. That sin would be recorded and brought to account on that day.

# Unforgiven sin will be judged

*1 John 5:16 "If anyone sees his brother sinning a sin not to death, he will ask, and He will give him life for those who commit sin not to death. There is sin to death. I do not say that he should pray about that."*

*John 8:34 "Jesus answered them, "Most assuredly, I say to you, whoever commits sin is a slave of sin."*

*2 Timothy 2:24-26 "And a servant of the Lord must not quarrel but be gentle to all, able to teach, patient, (25) in humility correcting those who are in opposition, if God perhaps will grant them repentance, so that they may know the truth, (26) and that they may come to their senses and escape the snare of the devil, having been taken captive by him to do his will."*

On this point, it is also very important that we keep a look out for our brothers and sisters in Christ. For when a believer falls into sin they become blinded by the god of this world, as they have now stepped into darkness. And so they become more and more oblivious to the sin that they are committing, thus not asking the Lord for forgiveness any longer. This is why scripture teaches us in one John chapter five quoted above, that if we see our brother committing sin not to death, that we should intercede to the Lord on their behalf, asking Him to forgive them their sin. That prayer has the same effect as if they themselves had asked the Lord's forgiveness. He immediately cleanses them of their sin and they once again can clearly see their sin, and themselves then repent and turn back to having fellowship with Him once more. Moses is a classic example given to us in scripture, of one who interceded to the Lord on behalf of the children on Israel, for their sins committed against Him. Time and again, our Lord listened to Moses prayer and forgave the children of Israel their sins, even though they were oblivious to the fact that they had come close to experiencing the judgement and wrath of God. Our Lord expects us to take the same role that Moses took, on behalf of our brothers and sisters in Christ. I know in my own life, that my wife and fellow believers prayed for me when I was in a backslidden state. And it was as a result of their prayers, that I was restored to fellowship with our Lord Jesus once again. Please note that I am not referring to isolated incidents of sin committed by the believer during their walk in this life, which they were negligent to confess before the Lord and ask His forgiveness. I am referring to a lifestyle, in which a believer habitually practices certain sins. The reason that they continually practice these sins, is because they have become enslaved to those sins. In John chapter eight quoted above, our Lord Jesus taught us that the one who commits sin, ultimately becomes enslaved by that sin. In two Timothy chapter two quoted above, the Holy Spirit through the apostle Paul, reveals that there are believers who have been taken captive by Satan to do his will. At one time, these believers walked free from sin, but opened the door to their adversary through sin, and subsequently became enslaved by that sin. The context of this comment made by Paul regarding these individuals, is that they had begun to teach heresy in the church. When we see a brother in the Lord committing sin, and we pray to the Lord to forgive them their sin and give them life, those sins are blotted out of heavens records by the precious blood of the Lamb. And those sins will not be remembered on that day.

*Matthew 12:32 "Anyone who speaks a word against the Son of Man, it will be forgiven him; but whoever speaks against the Holy Spirit, it will not be forgiven him, either in this age or in the age to come."*

*James 2:12-13 "So speak and so do as those who will be judged by the law of liberty. (13) For judgment is without mercy to the one who has shown no mercy. Mercy triumphs over judgment."*

*Revelation 21:4 "And God will wipe away every tear from their eyes; there shall be no more death, nor sorrow, nor crying. There shall be no more pain, for the former things have passed away."*

We have seen that sin that has forgiven us in this age, remains forgiven in the age to come. In Matthew chapter twelve quoted above, our Lord Jesus taught us that there are certain sins that are not forgiven in this age, or in the age to come. We know that one of the sins that are not forgiven in this age and the age to come, is the sin of rejecting Jesus as Lord and Saviour. In the passage of scripture quoted above, Jesus taught us that another sin that would not be forgiven in either this age or in the age to come, was the sin of blasphemy against the Holy Spirit. When our Lord taught us this truth, He also therefore implied that for the believer, there are sins that are not forgiven in this age, but which will be forgiven in the age to come. The sins that are not forgiven in this age but which will be forgiven in the age to come, are all unconfessed sins that believers commit in this age. The believers' sins which are not forgiven in this age and are yet forgiven in the age to come, will be forgiven solely through the mercy of the Lord Jesus on the Day of Judgment. As we have already seen in James chapter two quoted above, the Holy Spirit has shown us that mercy will be shown to the believers in their day of judgement. The reason for that is because all unconfessed sins must be forgiven, for there is no sin allowed in the kingdom of God. The sin of unforgiveness will be the first sin that will be dealt with on that day. For the scripture is plain when it tells us that unless we forgive others, then our Lord cannot forgive us. That principle applies, even in the age to come. There are many believers who have fallen asleep, while still holding onto unforgiveness toward others. Every believer who fell asleep while still holding onto this sin, will immediately forgive all others when they stand in the presence of their Lord on that day. As each unconfessed sin is revealed on that day, the believer will tearfully repent of each one, and ask the Lord's forgiveness. This is what the scripture means, when it says that some will be ashamed before Him on that day. In Revelations chapter twenty-one quoted above, the scripture reveals to us that God Himself, will wipe away every tear on that day. Our Lord Jesus, who is rich in mercy, will be merciful to His saints on that day, and forgive them their sins.

### Least in the kingdom

*Matthew 5:18-19 "For assuredly, I say to you, till heaven and earth pass away, one jot or one tittle will by no means pass from the law till all is fulfilled. (19) Whoever therefore breaks one of the least of these commandments, and teaches men so, shall be called least in the kingdom of heaven; but whoever does and teaches them, he shall be called great in the kingdom of heaven."*

*James 2:10-11 "For whoever shall keep the whole law, and yet stumble in one point, he is guilty of all. (11) For He who said, "do not commit adultery," also said, "do not murder." Now if you do not commit adultery, but you do murder, you have become a transgressor of the law."*

*2 Timothy 2:20-21 "But in a great house there are not only vessels of gold and silver, but also of wood and clay, some for honour and some for dishonour. (21) Therefore, if anyone cleanses himself from the latter, he will be a vessel for honour, sanctified and useful for the Master, prepared for every good work."*

Even though unforgiven sin in this age will be forgiven us through our Lord's mercy on that day, there will still be a price to pay. Our Lord Jesus said there would be. The price paid by believers, who continually break even the least of the Lord's commandments and teach others to do the same, is that those believers will be placed among those who are called least in the kingdom of heaven. Notice that in Matthew chapter five quoted above, that our Lord Jesus refers to the breaking of the least of His commandments, as cause to be called least in the kingdom of heaven. He is not then saying that those who break the greatest of His commandments will incur a greater penalty. Not at all. Because all of the commandments are His, and the one who transgresses even the least of His commandments has become a transgressor of His laws. In James chapter two quoted above, the Holy Spirit through the apostle James, teaches us this truth in that He tells us that when we commit just one sin, that we are then guilty of transgressing the whole law, not just one law. So, what is the eternal impact on the saint who is called least in the kingdom of heaven? The simple answer to that question is that they forgo their eternal inheritance. In two Timothy chapter two quoted above, the Holy Spirit through the apostle Paul, teaches us that in a great house there are vessels, both for honour and for dishonour. The context of His teaching in this passage of scripture is that certain individuals in the church had been teaching false doctrine, and Paul was commenting on their status in the kingdom of God, as a result of what they were teaching. Even though they were teaching false doctrine, they still remained in the house. The house in this passage of scripture refers to the kingdom of God. But because they had not cleansed themselves from dishonour, they would become vessels for dishonour in the kingdom of God. You will recall that on numerous occasions, our Lord Jesus taught us that many who are first in this life would be last in the age to come, and that many that are last in this life would be first in the age to come. In explaining this statement, Jesus said that those who wanted to be great in the kingdom of God, had to become servant of all in this life. Those who forgo their eternal inheritance because of a lifestyle of practising sin in this life, will not reign in the kingdom of God, but rather they will become servants in the kingdom

# Unforgiven sin will be judged

of God. It is in their inheritance that the saint who is called least in the kingdom of heaven, pays the price for their sin. They will be saved, but they will have no inheritance in the kingdom of God.

*1 Corinthians 6:8-10 "No, you yourselves do wrong and cheat, and you do these things to your brethren! (9) Do you not know that the unrighteous will not inherit the kingdom of God? Do not be deceived. Neither fornicators, nor idolaters, nor adulterers, nor homosexuals, nor sodomites, (10) nor thieves, nor covetous, nor drunkards, nor revilers, nor extortioners will inherit the kingdom of God."*

*1 Corinthians 5:11 "But now I have written to you not to keep company with anyone named a brother, who is sexually immoral, or covetous, or an idolater, or a reviler, or a drunkard, or an extortioner--not even to eat with such a person."*

*Galatians 5:19-21 "Now the works of the flesh are evident, which are: adultery, fornication, uncleanness, lewdness, (20) idolatry, sorcery, hatred, contentions, jealousies, outbursts of wrath, selfish ambitions, dissensions, heresies, (21) envy, murders, drunkenness, revelries, and the like; of which I tell you beforehand, just as I also told you in time past, that those who practice such things will not inherit the kingdom of God."*

On numerous occasions in the New Testament, the Holy Spirit warns believers that certain people will have no inheritance in the kingdom of God. The first time we are warned about this, is in Paul's letter to the church at Corinth. In one Corinthians chapter six quoted above, Paul is writing to believers, when he warns them about the loss of their eternal inheritance because of a lifestyle of practising sin. It is very important to note the terminology that the Holy Spirit uses here. He does not say that they will no longer be saved, and that they will now be condemned with the world because they are committing these sins. He specifically uses the term, that they will not inherit the kingdom of God. Because no matter how grievous these sins are, they are not the sin unto death. We know that the Holy Spirit is referring to believers in this passage of scripture, because as quoted above in the previous chapter, He counsels believers not to fellowship with brothers in Christ who are practicing those same sins listed. The second time that the Holy Spirit warns us about our eternal inheritance, is in His letter to the churches in Galatia, as quoted in Galatians chapter five above. Again, it is very important for us to note that the Holy Spirit uses the same terminology. He is emphasizing this point for us so that we can clearly see the truth that these individuals remain saved, but have no inheritance in the kingdom of God. Paul on this occasion, reminds the churches in Galatia that he had already forewarned them about the very same thing, when he was previously with them. And so, he warns them yet again, that believers who practice the sins listed, will have no inheritance in the kingdom of God. In this passage of scripture, the Holy Spirit is not warning those in the world who practice these sins, that they will not inherit the kingdom of God. He is clearly warning His church.

# Unforgiven sin will be judged

*Ephesians 5:1-7 "Therefore be imitators of God as dear children. (2) And walk in love, as Christ also has loved us and given Himself for us, an offering and a sacrifice to God for a sweet-smelling aroma. (3) But fornication and all uncleanness or covetousness, let it not even be named among you, as is fitting for saints; (4) neither filthiness, nor foolish talking, nor coarse jesting, which are not fitting, but rather giving of thanks. (5) For this you know, that no fornicator, unclean person, nor covetous man, who is an idolater, has any inheritance in the kingdom of Christ and God. (6) Let no one deceive you with empty words, for because of these things the wrath of God comes upon the sons of disobedience. (7) Therefore do not be partakers with them."*

*Colossians 3:4-25 "When Christ who is our life appears, then you also will appear with Him in glory. (5) Therefore put to death your members which are on the earth: fornication, uncleanness, passion, evil desire, and covetousness, which is idolatry. (6) Because of these things the wrath of God is coming upon the sons of disobedience, (7) in which you yourselves once walked when you lived in them. (8) But now you yourselves are to put off all these: anger, wrath, malice, blasphemy, filthy language out of your mouth. (9) Do not lie to one another, since you have put off the old man with his deeds, ... (23) And whatever you do, do it heartily, as to the Lord and not to men, (24) knowing that from the Lord you will receive the reward of the inheritance; for you serve the Lord Christ. (25) But he who does wrong will be repaid for what he has done, and there is no partiality."*

The third time that the Holy Spirit warns us about our eternal inheritance, is in His letter to the church in Ephesus, as quoted above in Ephesians chapter five. Again, it is very important for us to note that the Holy Spirit uses almost the exact same terminology. He is going to great lengths to show us that these individuals remain saved, but have no inheritance in the kingdom of God. In this letter, Paul again lists the sins that, if practiced by the believer, will cause them to lose their inheritance in the kingdom of God. In this letter, the Holy Spirit tells us that those in the world who practice these same sins will incur the wrath of God. And so, He admonishes us to not let anyone try deceive us, that these sins will not have any consequence for the believer. Because God is not unjust to punish the world with His wrath for these sins, and then let His saints commit the same sins and not be held to any account for those sins. The fourth time that the Holy Spirit warns the believers about their eternal inheritance, is when He writes to the church in Colossi, as quoted in Colossians chapter three above. Again, in this letter, Paul lists the sins that will cause the world to incur the wrath of God. He then admonishes the church not to partake of those self-same sins. The reason that we are admonished to not practice the same sins is because those in the church who do wrong will be repaid for those sins, and there is no partiality with our Lord, for He is a just God. As He does not tolerate those sins in the world and visits His wrath on those who commit them, He also does not tolerate those sins in His church and He will hold His saints to account for those same sins. The Holy Spirit, tells us that the one who serves the Lord from their spirit, can expect to receive the reward of their inheritance. But the Holy Spirit then also tells us that the one who chooses to do wrong, will be repaid for what he has done. In other words, they can expect to not receive the reward of their eternal inheritance.

*Hebrews 12:14-17 "Pursue peace with all people, and holiness, without which no one will see the Lord: (15) looking carefully lest anyone fall short of the grace of God; lest any root of bitterness springing up cause trouble, and by this many become defiled; (16) lest there be any fornicator or profane person like Esau, who for one morsel of food sold his birth right. (17) For you know that afterward, when he wanted to inherit the blessing, he was rejected, for he found no place for repentance, though he sought it diligently with tears."*

*Luke 16:9-12 "And I say to you, make friends for yourselves by unrighteous mammon, that when you fail, they may receive you into an everlasting home. (10) He who is faithful in what is least is faithful also in much; and he who is unjust in what is least is unjust also in much. (11) Therefore, if you have not been faithful in the unrighteous mammon, who will commit to your trust the true riches? (12) And if you have not been faithful in what is another man's, who will give you what is your own?"*

The scripture reveals to us that on the day of the saints' judgement that there will be tears, and that God

Himself will wipe away those tears. The reason that some saints will have tears on that day, is when they realize that they have forgone their eternal inheritance because of their chosen lifestyle that cheated them of their eternal rewards. The Holy Spirit gives us one more warning about losing our inheritance, when He writes to the church of the Hebrews, as quoted in Hebrews chapter twelve above. He reminds us about Esau, who for one morsel of food sold his birth right. Although Esau remained a son he had lost his inheritance, and when he finally realized his folly it was too late for him, and his inheritance could not be restored even though he sought it diligently with tears. The Holy Spirit warns us not to be like Esau and through sin, such as bitterness and fornication for example, give up our eternal inheritance. Our Lord Jesus, when He walked the earth, gave us a glimpse of one who was saved, but had lost their eternal inheritance. He did so through the parable of the unjust steward, quoted from Luke chapter sixteen above. At the end of the parable our Lord Jesus gives us some advice regarding our eternal inheritance. In that advice, He mentions an individual that will not have his own home in the age to come, but would be reliant on the grace of others to welcome him into their eternal homes. The reason that this individual had lost his own eternal home, was because he had been unjust in his lifestyle and had thus forfeited his eternal inheritance. In this same passage of scripture, our Lord also tells us that the one who is not faithful serving Him in this life, will not receive their inheritance in the age to come. For Jesus said that if we have not been faithful in what is another man's, who will give us what is our own? The other man He is referring to, is Himself. And that

# Unforgiven sin will be judged

which is our own which He is referring to, is our eternal inheritance.

*Luke 19:12-27 "Therefore He said: "A certain nobleman went into a far country to receive for himself a kingdom and to return. (13) So he called ten of his servants, delivered to them ten minas, and said to them, 'Do business till I come.' (14) But his citizens hated him, and sent a delegation after him, saying, 'We will not have this man to reign over us.' (15) "And so it was that when he returned, having received the kingdom, he then commanded these servants, to whom he had given the money, to be called to him, that he might know how much every man had gained by trading. (16) Then came the first, saying, 'Master, your mina has earned ten minas.' (17) And he said to him, 'Well done, good servant; because you were faithful in a very little, have authority over ten cities.' (18) And the second came, saying, 'Master, your mina has earned five minas.' (19) Likewise he said to him, 'You also be over five cities.' (20) "Then another came, saying, 'Master, here is your mina, which I have kept put away in a handkerchief. (21) For I feared you, because you are an austere man. You collect what you did not deposit, and reap what you did not sow.' (22) And he said to him, 'Out of your own mouth I will judge you, you wicked servant. You knew that I was an austere man, collecting what I did not deposit and reaping what I did not sow. (23) Why then did you not put my money in the bank, that at my coming I might have collected it with interest?' (24) "And he said to those who stood by, 'Take the mina from him, and give it to him who has ten minas.' (25) (But they said to him, 'Master, he has ten minas.') (26) 'For I say to you, that to everyone who has will be given; and from him who does not have, even what he has will be taken away from him. (27) But bring here those enemies of mine, who did not want me to reign over them, and slay them before me.'"*

In Luke chapter nineteen quoted above, our Lord Jesus taught us a parable regarding our day of judgement. In this parable, we see very clearly the principle that some on the day of judgement, will have no inheritance in His kingdom. In this parable, every servant received equally from their master when He went away. All saints when they come into the kingdom, receive the same gift of salvation along with the same measure of faith and grace. Most believers take their gift of salvation, and live lives as witnesses for their Master. As mentioned by the Lord, those servants will be rewarded on that day. But there are some believers who do not live lives worthy of their salvation, and will have no fruit to show on that day. On that day, those believers will give up their inheritance for others whom our Lord deems worthy. The servant who produced no fruit still remained in the kingdom, but they had no reward. And even that which they had, was taken away from them. You will recall that when our Lord taught the parable of the sower who sowed the seed, that there were those who produced thirtyfold, sixtyfold and some one hundredfold. That same principle applies in this parable, for the one servant produced tenfold while the other servant produced fivefold. In this parable, the one who produced nothing, can be likened to the one who produced no fruit from the seed sown, in the parable of the sower. The reason they produced no fruit in that parable, was because they allowed thorns to choke the word. The thorns were the cares of this life, the deceitfulness of riches and the lust of other things.

*Revelation 3:14-19 "And to the angel of the church of the Laodiceans write, 'These things says the Amen, the Faithful and True Witness, the Beginning of the creation of God: (15) "I know your works, that you are neither cold nor hot. I could wish you were cold or hot. (16) So then, because you are lukewarm, and neither cold nor hot, I will vomit you out of My mouth. (17) Because you say, 'I am rich, have become wealthy, and have need of nothing'-and do not know that you are wretched, miserable, poor, blind, and naked-- (18) I counsel you to buy from Me gold refined in the fire, that you may be rich; and white garments, that you may be clothed, that the shame of your nakedness may not be revealed; and anoint your eyes with eye salve, that you may see. (19) As many as I love, I rebuke and chasten. Therefore, be zealous and repent."*

In Revelation chapter three quoted above, the Lord Jesus revealed to us what inheritance awaited the church of Laodicea. It would benefit us to look at this graphic account that Lord gave us. In His letter, there were no believers whom the Lord commended in this particular church, for none of them were walking as they should. The believers in this church were walking in covetousness, because material wealth was all that mattered to them. There are two main things that are revealed to us in this passage of scripture, that I want to focus on. Firstly, even in their sinful state, our Lord still acknowledged them as being His children. They were borderline believers however, for they were very close to committing the sin to death, and thus being removed from the body of Christ. But at this time, they were still in His kingdom. Secondly, our Lord revealed their state as it existed in heaven at the time He spoke to them. He said to them that they were wretched, miserable, poor, blind and naked. In other words, they had no inheritance stored up for them in heaven. Unless these believers repented, their status would remain the same, and they would have no inheritance on their day of judgement. Our Lord couldn't make it any clearer than that. We are not to be deceived into thinking that no matter how we live our lives, that we will not be held to account on that day.

I will close off this chapter with an account of the following dream that our Lord Jesus gave to me regarding that which we have discussed in this chapter. The background to this dream is that I had been in a backslidden condition for a number of years, and as I briefly mentioned earlier, through the prayers of my wife and others, I was restored to fellowship once again with my Lord and Saviour. In my dream, I was standing between two men, and we were waiting our turn to stand before the judgment seat of Christ. There seemed to be a long queue winding up towards the judgment seat. The man on my right said, "well at least we are saved". He then disappeared. I knew instinctively that he had no works that he had done that the Lord would reward him for. Then the man on my left and I were standing before the throne. I standing to the side between the Lord and this man watching as this man was being judged. The man was

on my left and I was aware of Jesus standing on my right, but I did not see Him or look at Him. While we stood there, I heard the Lord speaking to the man on my left and He began to list the deeds that he should have done while he was on the earth. For each deed, He spoke about, He showed the reward that the Father had given Jesus to give to this man (I cannot describe the rewards but they were of great beauty. I do recall seeing a crown amongst the rewards). It was evident that this man had not done what the Lord had asked him to do. The Lord spoke in the following manner; "I spoke to you on this occasion and asked you to do this deed, or to speak to this person but you did not obey Me". I do not know the details of each time that this man had not been obedient to the Lord, but I know that I became more and more alarmed and concerned for the individual, as each account was mentioned. By the time the Lord had listed the fifth or sixth incident I could no longer restrain myself and I burst into tears of remorse for this individual, for my heart was broken for him. I then realised that the Lord was in fact dealing with me in the dream, and tearfully I repented before the Lord and asked His forgiveness for not having obeyed Him in my life as I ought to have done.
I then found myself walking back down from the throne, still in tears but now they were tears of joy. For I had joy in my heart knowing that my time had not yet come for me to stand before the judgment seat of Christ. And knowing that by the grace of God I still had time to be obedient to the Lord in what He had called me to do on the earth. Although the Lord was dealing with me in this dream the principle remains valid for all of us. We need to be obedient to what the Lord calls each of us to do on this

earth, and that it is not the Lord's will that we are just saved.

# Chapter 5

# Rewards available to the saints

## Rewards for the overcomer

*1 Peter 1:3-4 "Blessed be the God and Father of our Lord Jesus Christ, who according to His abundant mercy has begotten us again to a living hope through the resurrection of Jesus Christ from the dead, (4) to an inheritance incorruptible and undefiled and that does not fade away, reserved in heaven for you."*

*1 John 5:4-5 "For whatever is born of God overcomes the world. And this is the victory that has overcome the world--our faith. (5) Who is he who overcomes the world, but he who believes that Jesus is the Son of God?"*

*Revelation 12:11 "And they overcame him by the blood of the Lamb and by the word of their testimony, and they did not love their lives to the death."*

For the saints that remain true to the Lord Jesus and endure to the end of their time here on the earth, there are great rewards stored up for them in heaven. In first Peter chapter one quoted above, the Holy Spirit through the apostle Peter, reveals to us that our inheritance is reserved in heaven for us. He also reveals to us that our inheritance is incorruptible, undefiled and does not fade away. In other words, our inheritance is eternal. There are two categories of eternal rewards revealed to us in scripture. The first category, are the rewards that are the same for every saint. The only requirement given to us in scripture, in order to receive these particular rewards is that the saint must overcome in this life. In the book of Revelation, when our Lord Jesus spoke to each of the churches, He closed each of His addresses to those churches with the statement, "To him who overcomes". After each of these statements, our Lord then revealed one of the rewards that He has laid up in heaven for those who overcome. So, what are the qualities of a believer who overcomes? In one John chapter five quoted above, the Holy Spirit through the apostle John, reveals to us that he who overcomes is the one who is born of God. For those who are born of God, by faith overcome the world. And those who are born of God believe that Jesus is the Son of God. And so simply put, every believer overcomes the world, for every believer believes that Jesus is the Son of God, and every believer is born of God. In Revelation chapter twelve quoted above, the Holy Spirit through the apostle John, reveals to us that the overcoming believer is one who overcomes Satan, by being washed in the blood of the Lamb. They also overcome him by not being ashamed of the gospel of Jesus Christ, but freely share their faith in Jesus with others, even if it costs them their life to do so. Thus, everyone who is born-again, qualifies for the rewards listed by the Lord Jesus for the believer who overcomes. The reason for this, is because these particular rewards are freely given to us by Jesus Christ our Lord. Unlike the second category of rewards, these rewards cannot be earned. Each one is freely given to the church by the head of the church. Jesus does this, because He paid the price for these rewards with His own precious blood. These rewards were earned by the Lord Jesus for us, and are thus freely given to us, in Him.

*Revelation 2:7 "He who has an ear, let him hear what the Spirit says to the churches. To him who overcomes I will give to eat from the tree of life, which is in the midst of the Paradise of God."*

*Ezekiel 47:12 "Along the bank of the river, on this side and that, will grow all kinds of trees used for food; their leaves will not wither, and their fruit will not fail. They will bear fruit every month, because their water flows from the sanctuary. Their fruit will be for food, and their leaves for medicine."*

*Revelation 22:2 "In the middle of its street, and on either side of the river, was the tree of life, which bore twelve fruits, each tree yielding its fruit every month. The leaves of the tree were for the healing of the nations."*

*Genesis 3:22-24 "Then the LORD God said, "Behold, the man has become like one of Us, to know good and evil. And now, lest he put out his hand and take also of the tree of life, and eat, and live forever"- (23) therefore the LORD God sent him out of the garden of Eden to till the ground from which he was taken. (24) So, He drove out the man; and He placed cherubim at the east of the garden of Eden, and a flaming sword which turned every way, to guard the way to the tree of life."*

# Rewards available to the saints

So, let us now examine each of the rewards that our Lord will give to His saints, who overcome in this life. In Revelation chapter two quoted above, the first reward that our Lord Jesus lists for the one who overcomes, is that they will be allowed to eat from the tree of life. This tree of life is the same one that is referred to, in the book of Genesis. As this tree was physically present in the Garden of Eden, this tree will also be physically present in the New Jerusalem. In fact, as revealed to us in Ezekiel chapter forty-seven quoted above, this tree will also be present in the Jerusalem from which our Lord Jesus will reign, during His millennial reign on the earth. Notice that in Ezekiel's vision that the Lord showed him many trees, not just one. The tree of life produces twelve different fruits. It produces a different fruit each month of the year. In Revelation chapter twenty-two quoted above, the Holy Spirit through the apostle John, reveals to us just where the tree of life will be located in the new Jerusalem. The city of Jerusalem is set upon a mountain that is two thousand four hundred kilometres high. Winding down around the mountain, is the street of gold. In the middle of that street is the river of life flowing down from the throne of God and the Lamb. On either side of that river, the tree of life will be growing along its banks. Obviously, it is not just one tree but rather many trees, as revealed in Ezekiel's vision. As an aside, it is interesting to note that the new earth that God our Father creates will also orbit a new sun that He will create. For the new earth, will revolve around that sun on an axis that will take one year to complete. With regards to the fruit from the tree of life, the fruit of this tree will be food for our resurrected bodies, which makes them immortal. As revealed in Genesis chapter three quoted above, had Adam partaken of the tree of life in the garden of Eden, then his body would have become immortal. Which would have placed him in the class of angels, who can never die. That is why God had to remove Adam from the proximity of the tree of life, after he had sinned.  Only the saints of God who overcome, will have the right to eat of His tree of life.

*Revelation 2:11 "He who has an ear, let him hear what the Spirit says to the churches. He who overcomes shall not be hurt by the second death."*

*Revelation 20:10-15 "The devil, who deceived them, was cast into the lake of fire and brimstone where the beast and the false prophet are. And they will be tormented day and night forever and ever. ... (13) The sea gave up the dead who were in it, and Death and Hades delivered up the dead who were in them. And they were judged, each one according to his works.  (14)  Then Death and Hades were cast into the lake of fire. This is the second death.  (15) And anyone not found written in the Book of Life was cast into the lake of fire."*

*Matthew 25:41 "Then He will also say to those on the left hand, 'Depart from Me, you cursed, into the everlasting fire prepared for the devil and his angels."*

As quoted above from Revelation chapter two, the second reward that our Lord Jesus has for the one who overcomes, is that they will not be hurt by the second death. So what is the second death? Scripture quoted from

# Rewards available to the saints

Revelation chapter twenty above, reveals to us that the second death is a lake of fire that burns for all eternity. That same scripture reveals to us that those whose names are not recorded in the Book of Life, are destined to experience the second death. Every man born into the earth, originally have their names recorded in the book of life, for it was never God's intention that any man should experience the second death. But those who choose to reject salvation through Jesus Christ our Lord eventually have their names blotted out of the book of life, when they physically die. All of God's enemies will be cast into that lake. At the final judgment, even those who are currently being held in Hades, will be taken out of Hell to receive their final judgment and be cast into this lake. Scripture reveals to us that the Anti-Christ and the false prophet will be cast alive into this lake of fire, when our Lord Jesus returns to reign on the earth for one thousand years. In fact, these two individuals will be the first to be cast into that lake of fire. Scripture also reveals to us that Satan and his angels will be cast into this lake of fire and brimstone, because ultimately God prepared the lake of fire for Satan and his angels, as revealed to us by the Lord in Matthew chapter twenty-five quoted above. God never intended that men should have ended up there. However, many have followed after Satan and rejected salvation through Jesus Christ our Lord, and so regrettably they too will be cast into the lake of fire along with the god of this world. As we have seen in in the scripture quoted above, Death and Hades themselves, will eventually be cast into this lake of fire. There, all will suffer torment for all eternity. Scripture also reveals to us that this lake of fire will be located just outside the city walls of the new Jerusalem, and that we will be able to see the torment of those who

# Rewards available to the saints

have rebelled against God. The scripture also reveals to us
that the smoke of their torment will be seen rising from
that lake, for all eternity. Our Lord Jesus reveals to us that
this second death has no power over us, as His saints.

*Revelation 2:17 "He who has an ear, let him
hear what the Spirit says to the churches. To him
who overcomes I will give some of the hidden manna
to eat."*

*John 6:31-35 "Our fathers ate the manna in the
desert; as it is written, 'He gave them bread from
heaven to eat.'" (32) Then Jesus said to them, "Most
assuredly, I say to you, Moses did not give you the
bread from heaven, but My Father gives you the true
bread from heaven. (33) For the bread of God is He
who comes down from heaven and gives life to the
world." (34) Then they said to Him, "Lord, give us
this bread always." (35) And Jesus said to them, "I
am the bread of life. He who comes to Me shall never
hunger, and he who believes in Me shall never thirst."*

*Psalms 78:24-25 "Had rained down manna on
them to eat, and given them of the bread of heaven.
(25) Men ate angels' food; He sent them food to the
full."*

*1 Corinthians 10:3-4 "all ate the same spiritual
food, (4) and all drank the same spiritual drink. For
they drank of that spiritual Rock that followed them,
and that Rock was Christ."*

In Revelation chapter two quoted above, the third reward that our Lord Jesus has for the one who overcomes, is that He will give them some of the hidden manna to eat. So just what is the hidden manna that our Lord Jesus promises us? As quoted from John chapter six above, when Jesus was on the earth, the Jews disputed with Him about the fact that Moses had given them manna from heaven to eat. Jesus then taught them that He indeed was the true manna from heaven, in that He was the bread of life. We do know that the manna that the children of Israel ate in the wilderness, was of the food that angels in heaven, eat. This truth is revealed to us in Psalm seventy-eight quoted above. In one Corinthians chapter ten quoted above, the Holy Spirit through the apostle Paul, refers to the manna that the children of Israel ate, as spiritual food. When He calls it spiritual food, we know that He is referring to the physical manna that they ate. Because in the same passage of scripture, He refers to the water that they drank from the rock, as spiritual drink. Spiritual food nourishes the spirit of man. As the fruit from the tree of life will be food to our resurrected bodies, so the hidden manna that our Lord Jesus will give us, will be food for our spirits. We know that here on earth, that by faith we feed our spirits with the word of God. And our Lord has taught us that man's spirit needs the word of God, in order to be able to live. The physical manna that the children of Israel ate, came from the very mouth of God. What form this hidden manna will take in heaven, is not yet revealed to us. But we have been shown on two separate occasions in scripture, where God has fed His servants His word, literally. The first account is when God gave the prophet Ezekiel the scroll to eat, as recorded in Ezekiel chapter two. The second account that we see in scripture, is when our Lord gave the apostle John a little book to eat, as recorded in Revelation chapter ten. Whatever form the hidden manna, that our Lord Jesus will give us takes, it will be nourishment for our spirits, as His word currently is.

*Revelation 2:17 "He who has an ear, let him hear what the Spirit says to the churches. To him who overcomes I will give some of the hidden manna to eat. And I will give him a white stone, and on the stone a new name written which no one knows except him who receives it."*

*Genesis 17:5 "No longer shall your name be called Abram, but your name shall be Abraham; for I have made you a father of many nations."*

*Psalms 147:4 "He counts the number of the stars; He calls them all by name."*

As revealed to us in Revelation chapter two quoted above, the fourth reward that our Lord Jesus has for the one who overcomes, is that He will give to each one a white stone on which is written their new name. On earth, our parents named each one of us. Each name has its own meaning, and should describe the character of that person. We have seen in scripture where individuals had their names changed by God, when He called them to follow Him. In Genesis chapter seventeen quoted above, we see that before God changed Abrams name, his name meant "father". After God changed his name, his new name Abraham, meant "father of many nations". And so, we see that God called Abraham by the name that described who he had become, or more accurately, who God had made him to be. On that day, each one of us will receive our new name, given to us by our heavenly Father. The names that our Lord Jesus will give us will be unique to each one of us. Unlike here on earth, no saint will receive a name that another saint is also named by. I have heard of people who have prophesied over others as to what their names will be in heaven, and invariably the names prophesied are those we have all heard of before. I just smile, because I know that these people are just speaking out of their flesh, for the Holy Spirit does not violate the word of God. In Psalm one hundred and forty-seven quoted above, the scripture tells us that God names each one of the stars in the universe, individually. And there are well over one billion trillion stars in the observable universe. Each one of us will receive our own unique name from the Lord Jesus. And only God and the individual will know that name. And that name will describe how God sees each one of us, and who He has made us to be.

*Revelation 2:26-27 "And he who overcomes, and keeps My works until the end, to him I will give power over the nations-- (27) 'he shall rule them with a rod of iron; they shall be dashed to pieces like the potter's vessels'-- as I also have received from My Father."*

*Revelation 20:4 "And I saw thrones, and they sat on them, and judgment was committed to them. Then I saw the souls of those who had been beheaded*

# Rewards available to the saints

*for their witness to Jesus and for the word of God,
who had not worshiped the beast or his image, and
had not received his mark on their foreheads or on
their hands. And they lived and reigned with Christ
for a thousand years."*

As revealed in Revelation chapter two quoted above,
the fifth reward that our Lord has for those who
overcome, is that He will give them power to rule over the
nations. There are two rewards listed for those who
overcome, which have another condition attached. In
other words, these rewards are not just for the ones who
overcome. This particular reward falls into that category.
Notice that in order to qualify for this reward that the
believer must overcome, but that they must also do
something else. Our Lord said that they must also keep
His works until the end. The saints that have been
practising sin, as we discussed in an earlier chapter, will
not qualify for this reward, as they would not have been
keeping our Lords works while they were on the earth.
You will recall that the Holy Spirit revealed to us, that
those believers would have no inheritance in the kingdom
of God. Part of our inheritance, is to rule over the nations.
Those saints will not rule over the nations, as they will
have no inheritance. However, for the saints that
overcome and have been keeping the Lord works on the
earth, their reward will be to rule over the nations. The
nations that we will rule over, will be the unbelieving
nations that are left on the earth when we return with our
Lord Jesus at His second coming. This event will occur
after the wrath of God has been poured out on the earth.
When our Lord Jesus returns to the earth He will destroy
the anti-Christ, along with all his followers as part of the

fourth kingdom. But scripture reveals to us that the three remaining kingdoms, will still be on the earth when our Lord returns. At that time, our Lord will also lock up Satan and his angels in the bottomless pit for one thousand years. (For a more detailed account of this period see my book "Resurrection of the Dead"). The nations that will be residing on the earth at that time will not be believers, as they would not have accepted Christ as their Saviour, prior to His return. As revealed in Revelation chapter twenty above, it is during the thousand-year reign of Christ that we, as His kings and representatives, will rule over these nations. It is estimated that there will be roughly six billion people living on the earth when we return with our Lord. Notice that we will rule over them with a rod of iron. Although the unbelieving nations will be in awe of the Lord Jesus and His saints, they will not always willingly submit to His rule. For they will still be spiritually dead people, and thus carnal in their thinking. To give you an example, in Zechariah chapter fourteen, the Holy Spirit reveals to us that all nations will be required to observe the feast of Tabernacles during that period. However, not all nations will always observe the feast of Tabernacles every year, as commanded by the Lord. When those nations rebel, then they will pay the price by incurring the Lord's punishment. That rod of iron will be very real.

*Revelation 2:26-28 "And he who overcomes, and keeps My works until the end, to him I will give power over the nations-- ... (28) and I will give him the morning star."*

# Rewards available to the saints

*Revelation 22:16 "I, Jesus, have sent My angel to testify to you these things in the churches. I am the Root and the Offspring of David, the Bright and Morning Star."*

*2 Peter 1:19 "And so we have the prophetic word confirmed, which you do well to heed as a light that shines in a dark place, until the day dawns and the morning star rises in your hearts."*

Again, in Revelation chapter two quoted above, we see the sixth reward listed that our Lord Jesus has for those who overcome. The reward our Lord mentions, is that He will give us the morning star. As revealed in Revelation chapter twenty-two quoted above, Jesus is the morning star, and so ultimately, He will give us of Himself, on that day. In two Peter chapter one quoted above, the Holy Spirit through the apostle Peter, teaches us that the morning star will rise in our hearts on that day. When Peter mentions that the morning star will rise in our hearts he means that we will be just like Jesus on that day, for we will see Him as He is.

*Revelation 3:5 "He who overcomes shall be clothed in white garments, and I will not blot out his name from the Book of Life; but I will confess his name before My Father and before His angels."*

*Revelation 7:13-14 "Then one of the elders answered, saying to me, "Who are these arrayed in white robes, and where did they come from?" (14) And I said to him, "Sir, you know." So he said to me,*

*"These are the ones who come out of the great tribulation, and washed their robes and made them white in the blood of the Lamb."*

*Revelation 19:8 "And to her it was granted to be arrayed in fine linen, clean and bright, for the fine linen is the righteous acts of the saints."*

In Revelation chapter three quoted above, it is revealed that the seventh reward that our Lord has for those who overcome, is that they will be clothed in white garments. Their names will not be blotted out from the book of life, and Jesus will confess their names before the Father and before His angels. In revelation chapter seven quoted above, we learn from scripture that we, as the saints of God, will all receive white garments on that day. Our garments will be white because we would have washed them in the blood of the Lamb. We also learn in Revelation chapter nineteen quoted above, that our white garments will reflect all of our righteous acts that we have done in Jesus, while on the earth. In that passage of scripture, the Holy Spirit describes the bride of Christ, by telling us that we will wear clean and bright linen, which are the righteous acts of the saints. In His letters to the churches in the book of Revelation, our Lord mentions the saints' garments twice. In His letter to the church in Sardis, He implied that there were those who had already defiled their garments. For He went on to say that some of the saints in that church had not defiled their garments, and that they would walk with Him in white, for they were worthy. It was to this church that our Lord then made the comment about those who overcome not having their names blotted out of the book of life, and of Him confessing their names before the Father and the angels in heaven. Obviously, the ones in Sardis who had defiled their garments, already had their names blotted out of the book of life and they would be denied before the Father on that day. The reason for that, was that these believers had committed the sin to death, thus defiling their garments. The second time our Lord mentioned the saints' garments was in His letter to the church in Laodicea. In that instance, our Lord informed them that they had no garments, and that they were in fact naked. The reason they had no garments, was because they had done no righteous acts. As believers, we are required to do works befitting righteousness, so that we may be clothed with white garments on that day. But, we must also be careful not to follow the path of the believers in Sardis, who had defiled their garments. For those are the ones who had their names blotted out of the book of life, and they will be denied by the Lord Jesus on that day.

*Revelation 3:12 "He who overcomes, I will make him a pillar in the temple of My God, and he shall go out no more. I will write on him the name of My God and the name of the city of My God, the New Jerusalem, which comes down out of heaven from My God. And I will write on him My new name."*

*Revelation 7:15 "Therefore they are before the throne of God, and serve Him day and night in His temple. And He who sits on the throne will dwell among them."*

*Revelation 7:2-3 "Then I saw another angel ascending from the east, having the seal of the living*

*God. And he cried with a loud voice to the four angels to whom it was granted to harm the earth and the sea, (3) saying, "Do not harm the earth, the sea, or the trees till we have sealed the servants of our God on their foreheads."*

In revelation chapter three quoted above, the eighth reward mentioned that our Lord will give to the one who overcomes, is that our Lord will make them a pillar in the temple of God and they shall go out of His temple no more. To be a pillar in the temple of God, means that we will abide in the presence of God throughout all eternity. In Revelation chapter seven quoted above, the scripture reveals to us that we will serve God day and night in His temple. Remember that our Lord Jesus has made us to be both kings and priests unto God our Father. Not only will we reign with Him throughout eternity as kings, but we will also minister to Him as priests throughout eternity. Our priestly roles will be to offer spiritual sacrifices before the Lord daily in His temple. There can be no greater honour bestowed on the people of God, than to worship before His throne in His very presence. Words in this life, cannot describe the glory that we will experience as His priests, worshipping before the throne of Majesty. Our Lord Jesus told us that He will also write on us the name of His God, the name of the city of His God and our Lord's new name. To have God's name and Jesus new name and the name of the city of God written on us, means that we will have the eternal seal of God placed upon us, as belonging to Him for all eternity. In Revelation chapter seven quoted above, the Holy Spirit reveals to us that the one hundred and forty-four thousand were sealed by the angel on their foreheads, just before they went into the

# Rewards available to the saints

period of God's wrath being poured out on the earth. The reason that they were sealed in this manner, was so that none of the plagues incurred by the earth would be able to come near them. All, for all eternity, will recognise those who belong to God, for we will have His name, the name of His Son and the name of His city written on us. That privilege will be ours for all eternity. We have no concept of the glories in store for the saints of God, throughout eternity.

*Revelation 3:21 "To him who overcomes I will grant to sit with Me on My throne, as I also overcame and sat down with My Father on His throne."*

*Romans 8:16-17 "The Spirit Himself bears witness with our spirit that we are children of God, (17) and if children, then heirs--heirs of God and joint heirs with Christ, if indeed we suffer with Him, that we may also be glorified together."*

As revealed in Revelation chapter three quoted above, the ninth reward that our Lord will give to the one who overcomes, is that He will grant them to sit with Jesus on His throne. But as we have already mentioned earlier, there are two rewards listed for those who overcome, which have another condition attached. This is the other reward that falls into that category. Notice that in order to qualify for this reward, that the believer must overcome, as our Lord Jesus overcame. So, what does the Lord mean when He tells us that this reward is available to the saint who overcomes, as He overcame? God our Father exalted our Lord Jesus to His own right hand,

# Rewards available to the saints

because Jesus was obedient to death, even the death of the cross. The scripture teaches us that our Lord learned obedience through the things which He suffered, including His death on the cross. In Romans chapter eight quoted above, the Holy Spirit through the apostle Paul, teaches us that if we want to reign with Christ, then the requirement is that we are going to have to suffer with Him. The apostle Peter teaches us that he who has suffered in the flesh, has ceased from sin. The saints that have been practising sin, as we discussed in an earlier chapter, will not qualify for this reward, as they would not have overcome as Jesus did. For they would have chosen to forgo suffering in the flesh. To be seated with Christ on His throne is the highest honour that God can bestow upon us, His children. This is what scripture means when it declares that we are joint heirs with Christ. As joint heirs with Christ we are to be seated together with Him in the heavenly places. All things have been placed under the feet of Christ. And as we sit together with Christ on His throne, all things will be placed under our feet and we will reign with Him for all eternity. In this present age, we reign with Christ by faith, but in the age to come we will experience the full reality of being seated together with Christ on His throne.

## Rewards that can be earned

*Mark 10:40 "but to sit on My right hand and on My left, is not Mine to give, but it is for those for whom it is prepared."*

*Matthew 19:28 "So Jesus said to them, "Assuredly I say to you, that in the regeneration,*

# Rewards available to the saints

*when the Son of Man sits on the throne of His glory,
you who have followed Me will also sit on twelve
thrones, judging the twelve tribes of Israel."*

*Psalms 122:3-7 "Jerusalem is built as a city
that is compact together, (4) Where the tribes go up,
the tribes of the LORD, To the Testimony of Israel, to
give thanks to the name of the LORD. (5) For
thrones are set there for judgment, The thrones of the
house of David. (6) Pray for the peace of Jerusalem:
"May they prosper who love you. (7) Peace be
within your walls, Prosperity within your palaces."*

This now brings us to the second category of
rewards that are laid up in heaven, for the saints. As with
the two conditional rewards mentioned earlier, I again
need to mention that the saints who live a lifestyle of
practicing sin will be excluded from these rewards as well,
for they have no inheritance in the kingdom of God. For
the rest of us, these rewards will differ for every saint, for
they are the rewards given based on our works done on
the earth. These rewards mainly consist of crowns given,
along with their related thrones of authority. These
rewards also consist of the treasures that have been stored
up, and accumulated for us in heaven. With regards to the
reward of reigning with Christ that we spoke about in the
previous section, not all saints will reign with the same
degree of authority. There will be differing levels of
authority given to His saints, based on their works done in
this life. As quoted above from Mark's gospel chapter ten,
you will recall that James and John had requested from
the Lord Jesus, that He would grant them to sit on His
right hand and His left, in His kingdom. He then informed

them that these particular positions of authority would be given to those for whom the Father had prepared them. In Matthew chapter nineteen quoted above, our Lord also clearly tells us that the apostles of the Lamb will have a specific level of authority in the kingdom of God. For He tells us that they will sit on thrones and judge the twelve tribes of Israel. Not all saints will have that level of authority given to them, on that day. And so, we see that the rewards that can be earned, relate to thrones that will be given. In Psalm one hundred and twenty-two quoted above, the Holy Spirit reveals to us that the thrones given, will be set in the city of Jerusalem, from which those who are appointed, will reign over the kingdom of God. As I have already stated, these thrones are also linked to crowns. For the one who sits on the throne, is crowned with the authority allocated to that throne.

*2 Timothy 4:8 "Finally, there is laid up for me the crown of righteousness, which the Lord, the righteous Judge, will give to me on that Day, and not to me only but also to all who have loved His appearing."*

*James 1:12 "Blessed is the man who endures temptation; for when he has been approved, he will receive the crown of life which the Lord has promised to those who love Him."*

*Revelation 2:10 "Do not fear any of those things which you are about to suffer. Indeed, the devil is about to throw some of you into prison, that you may be tested, and you will have tribulation ten*

# Rewards available to the saints

*days. Be faithful until death, and I will give you the crown of life.”*

*1 Peter 5:1-4 “The elders who are among you I exhort, I who am a fellow elder and a witness of the sufferings of Christ, and also a partaker of the glory that will be revealed: (2) Shepherd the flock of God which is among you, serving as overseers, not by compulsion but willingly, not for dishonest gain but eagerly; (3) nor as being lords over those entrusted to you, but being examples to the flock; (4) and when the Chief Shepherd appears, you will receive the crown of glory that does not fade away.”*

The scriptures reveal a number of different crowns that will be given to the Lord's saints, in that day. In two Timothy chapter four quoted above, the Holy Spirit through the apostle Paul, tells us about the crown of righteousness that is available for the Lord's saints in that day. Paul tells us that the saints that have loved our Lord's appearing, will qualify to receive this crown on that day. In James chapter one quoted above, the Holy Spirit through the apostle James, tells us about the crown of life that is available to the Lord's saints on that day. James tells us that the saint who endures temptation in this life and who loves the Lord, qualifies to receive this crown on that day. In Revelation chapter two quoted above, our Lord Jesus mentions the same crown, when He speaks to the church at Smyrna. Our Lord also tells us that the saint who endures testing and tribulation in this life even to the point of death, qualifies to receive this crown on that day. In one Peter chapter five quoted above, the Holy Spirit through the apostle Peter, tells us about the crown of glory that is available to the Lord's elders and shepherds, on that day. Peter tells us that the elders that serve willingly, and lead as examples to the Lord's flock, will qualify to receive that crown on that day. The point is that all of these crowns, (and I am sure that there many others) are available to the Lord's saints, as rewards on that day. Crowns are very important in the kingdom of God. In the book of Revelation chapter nineteen, the bible describes our Lord as one who has many crowns. The twenty-four elders that sit on thrones around the throne of God, all wear crowns of gold. None of the Lord's saints will be able to reign in the age to come, unless they receive their crown from Him.

*1 Corinthians 9:24-26 "Do you not know that those who run in a race all run, but one receives the prize? Run in such a way that you may obtain it. (25) And everyone who competes for the prize is temperate in all things. Now they do it to obtain a perishable crown, but we for an imperishable crown. (26) Therefore, I run thus: not with uncertainty. Thus, I fight: not as one who beats the air."*

*Revelation 3:11 "Behold, I am coming quickly! Hold fast what you have, that no one may take your crown."*

But none of the crowns available to the saints as rewards, are freely given. These are the rewards that are earned. And they are earned by the good works done by the saints, while they reside on the earth. In one Corinthians chapter nine quoted above, the Holy Spirit through the apostle Paul, encourages us to be focused in

# Rewards available to the saints

this life, so that we may receive the reward of our crown on that day. Paul tells us that we should run our race in such a way, that we may obtain our crowns. The analogy that he uses to describe how we should go about obtaining our crowns, is that of an athlete who competes in a race, in order to win that race. The athlete that is going to win their race, is the athlete that is disciplined in their preparation for their race. Our eternal crowns will not just fall into our laps by chance. They will be given to the saints that are determined to do what they need to do, in order to obtain them. But just as these rewards can be earned, so they can also be given up. In writing to the church in Philadelphia, as quoted above in Revelation chapter three, our Lord Jesus informed them that they had already received their crown, and that it was laid up for them in heaven. But He also admonished them to hold fast to what they had, and ensure that no one took their crown away from them.

*Psalms 48:12-13 "Walk about Zion, and go all around her. Count her towers; (13) Mark well her bulwarks; Consider her palaces; That you may tell it to the generation following."*

*Isaiah 65:21 "They shall build houses and inhabit them; They shall plant vineyards and eat their fruit."*

*2 Kings 5:26 "Then he said to him, "Did not my heart go with you when the man turned back from his chariot to meet you? Is it time to receive money and to receive clothing, olive groves and vineyards, sheep and oxen, male and female servants?"*

All of the crowns mentioned, and the many others, are linked to thrones of authority in the kingdom of God. Those who receive crowns and thrones of authority, will also receive palaces in the new Jerusalem. In Psalm forty-eight quoted above, the Holy Spirit through the psalmist, reveals this truth to us when He describes the palaces in the new Jerusalem. You will recall that Psalm one hundred and twenty-two quoted earlier, also mentioned the palaces of the saints in the new Jerusalem. Not only will the Lord's saints receive palaces in the new Jerusalem, but they will also receive lands and houses in the new earth that God will create. In Isaiah chapter sixty-five quoted above, the Holy Spirit through the prophet Isaiah, reveals this to us when He speaks about the new heavens and the new earth that God will create. For He tells us that we shall build houses to live in, and plant vineyards from which we will eat their fruit. Again, in two Kings chapter five quoted above, the Holy Spirit through the prophet Elisha, confirms the fact that those who serve the Lord in this age, will be rewarded in the age to come, with olive groves, vineyards, sheep, oxen, male and female servants. In the discourse that Elisha has with his servant Gehazi, Elisha reveals this truth to us. The context of the passage of scripture is that Elisha's servant had coveted material rewards from Naaman the Syrian, who the Lord had healed through Elisha's ministry. And so Gehazi had taken rewards from Naaman and hidden them from the prophet. But God had revealed to Elisha what Gehazi had done, and He used Elisha to judge Gehazi with leprosy. However, the point that I wanted to make from this passage of scripture, is that Elisha referred to the rewards awaiting the Lord's saints, in the age to come.

*Revelation 21:24-26 "And the nations of those who are saved shall walk in its light, and the kings of the earth bring their glory and honour into it. (25) Its gates shall not be shut at all by day (there shall be no night there). (26) And they shall bring the glory and the honour of the nations into it."*

*1 Kings 4:7 "And Solomon had twelve governors over all Israel, who provided food for the king and his household; each one made provision for one month of the year."*

In revelation chapter twenty-one quoted above, the Holy Spirit through the apostle John, reveals to us that the nations that live outside the city of Jerusalem in God's new earth, will bring their glory and honour into that city. I will not go into detail here, regarding the nations that will be living outside the city of Jerusalem, because that falls outside the scope of this teaching. Suffice it to say, that there will be nations living outside of the city walls in that day. The glory and honour of the kings of the earth that will be brought into the new Jerusalem, as revealed to us in the book of Revelation, will be the produce of the lands in God's new earth. The kingdom of Solomon was a type and shadow of God's kingdom, that will be on the earth in the age to come. In one Kings chapter four quoted above, we read how the nation of Israel provided for the city of Jerusalem, under the reign of Solomon. Solomon appointed twelve governors over the nation. Each of those governors were given one of the twelve months of the year, in which their region was to supply the needs of the city. As the city of Jerusalem was provided for by the children of Israel at that time, so the new Jerusalem will be provided for by the nations of those who are saved and dwelling in God's new earth. There is much more that we can talk about concerning the rewards awaiting the saints in the kingdom of God, including our priestly functions that we will perform, but that falls outside the scope of this teaching and so we will end this chapter here.

# Chapter 6

# Ministry gifts judgement

## Their judgement will be different

*Ephesians 4:11 "And He Himself gave some to be apostles, some prophets, some evangelists, and some pastors and teachers."*

*Galatians 1:15-16 "But when it pleased God, who separated me from my mother's womb and called me through His grace, (16) to reveal His Son in me, that I might preach Him among the Gentiles, I did not immediately confer with flesh and blood."*

*Philippians 4:1 "Therefore, my beloved and longed-for brethren, my joy and crown, so stand fast in the Lord, beloved."*

In this chapter, we will look at the judgment that those who are called to the ministry, can expect on that day. The reason that I have dedicated a separate chapter to their judgment, is because their judgement will be very different to the saints' judgement. In Ephesians chapter four quoted above, we see that the ministry gifts received from the Lord Jesus, are the gifts of apostle, prophet, evangelist, pastor and teacher. There are other ministry gifts mentioned in the bible, but these five are the main ministry gifts. As revealed in Galatians chapter one quoted above, all ministry gifts are separated to the Lord from the time they come into the earth. They may only answer their call very much later in life, as in the case of the apostle Paul, but nevertheless God chooses them to be ministers of His gospel before they are born, and they have no choice in the matter. The eternal work done in the lives of believers that these gifts have ministered to, will result in these ministry gifts being rewarded with their relevant crowns being given to them on that day. You will recall that earlier we looked at the scripture, where Paul spoke about how the ministry gifts built the Lord's house with silver, gold and precious stones. The silver, gold and precious stones that he was referring to, was the saints themselves. In Philippians chapter four quoted above, the apostle Paul stated that the believers that he had ministered to, would be his crown on that day. We saw in an earlier quoted scripture, that the apostle Peter stated that those called to shepherd the flock of God and were faithful in their ministries, would receive the crown of glory on that day.

*Mark 10:29-31 "So Jesus answered and said, "Assuredly, I say to you, there is no one who has left house or brothers or sisters or father or mother or wife or children or lands, for My sake and the gospel's, (30) who shall not receive a hundredfold now in this time--houses and brothers and sisters and mothers and children and lands, with persecutions--and in the age to come, eternal life. (31) But many who are first will be last, and the last first."*

*1 Corinthians 4:9 "For I think that God has displayed us, the apostles, last, as men condemned to death; for we have been made a*

*spectacle to the world, both to angels and to men."*
*Mark 9:35 "And He sat down, called the twelve, and*
*said to them, "If anyone desires to be first, he shall be*
*last of all and servant of all."*

You will recall that our Lord Jesus, on numerous occasions in His earthly ministry, spoke of those who are last being first and those who are first being last, on that day. When He made this comment, it was mainly in relation to those who would be called by Him, to the ministry of His gospel. In Mark chapter ten quoted above, we have an example of our Lord making that comment, and we can see that He made it in relation to His ministry gifts. Of all the ministry gifts, the ministry gift of apostle is the one that is the most important to the body of Christ (for more detail on this point see my book "The Five Ministry Gifts"). If you study scripture you will see that when our Lord Jesus mentioned the gift of the apostle, He always mentioned it first in relation to the other ministry gifts, and there is a reason for that. When I say that this ministry gift is the most important to the church, I am not speaking in worldly terms of importance. What I mean, is that the anointing placed on this gift is greater than the other ministry gifts and as such, has the potential to have the greatest impact on the church. In that light, now look at the comment made by the apostle Paul, regarding the ministry gift of the apostle, as quoted above from one Corinthians chapter four. It is God's intention that His apostles be displayed last in this age, as the servants of all, so that He can reward them as first, in the age to come. For you will recall that our Lord stated that those who wanted to be first in the age to come, had to be servant of all in this present age. We see this quoted above, in Mark chapter nine. Sadly, not all of the Lord's apostles live up to that call of being the servant of all. Nevertheless, the point remains that it is God's intention that His ministry gifts should be servants to His body, as examples to the rest of us. He does this so that he can reward them as being first, in the age to come.

*Ephesians 4:7 "But to each one of us grace was given according to the measure of Christ's gift."*

*Luke 12:48 "For everyone to whom much is given, from him much will be required; and to whom much has been committed, of him they will ask the more."*

*1 Corinthians 9:16-17 "For if I preach the gospel, I have nothing to boast of, for necessity is laid upon me; yes, woe is me if I do not preach the gospel! (17) For if I do this willingly, I have a reward; but if against my will, I have been entrusted with a stewardship."*

As much as the ministry gifts will be rewarded by the Lord for being faithful in their ministries, so there is a strong word of warning given to those called to the ministry, if they are not faithful in their ministries. As quoted in Ephesians chapter four above, every member in the body of Christ has received grace from Him, according to the measure of the gift He has given them. The ministry gifts receive a greater measure of grace, because their gifts are greater. In Luke chapter twelve quoted above, our Lord Jesus tells the ministry gifts that because they have been given much, that they will be required to account for more. In other words, they have received more grace than their brothers and sisters in Christ, and because of this they will be held to a higher degree of account, on that day. We saw earlier as quoted in James chapter three, that the Holy Spirit warns believers about becoming teachers in the church, because of the stricter judgement that they will incur on that day. Obviously when the Holy Spirit mentions this, He is not referring to those whom the Lord has called to the ministry gift of teacher in His church, for they have no choice in the matter. But the point remains, that the ministry gifts will receive a stricter judgement than their brothers and sisters, on that day. In one Corinthians chapter nine quoted above, the apostle Paul stated that he would experience grief if he did not preach the gospel. The reason Paul said this, is because he understood that Jesus is the one who called him to the ministry, and that he would stand before Jesus on that day to give an account of his ministry. Paul knew that this was a very serious issue that had eternal ramifications, and he took his ministry calling very seriously. The Lord's ministers need to take their callings seriously. To whom much is given much is required.

## Their judgement will be stricter

*Luke 12:41-48 "Then Peter said to Him, "Lord, do You speak this parable only to us, or to all people?" (42) And the Lord said, "Who then is that faithful and wise steward, whom his master will make ruler over his household, to give them their portion of food in due season? (43) Blessed is that servant whom his master will find so doing when he comes. (44) Truly, I say to you that he will make him ruler over all that he has. ... (47) And that servant who knew his master's will, and did not prepare himself or do according to his will, shall be beaten with many stripes. (48) But he who did not know, yet committed things deserving of stripes, shall be beaten with few. For everyone to whom much is given, from him much will be required; and to whom much has been committed, of him they will ask the more."*

*Psalms 89:27-32 "Also I will make him My firstborn, The highest of the kings of the earth. (28) My mercy I will keep for him forever, And My covenant shall stand firm with him. (29) His seed also I will make to endure forever, And his throne as the days of heaven. (30) "If his sons forsake My law and do not walk in My judgments, (31) If they break My statutes and do not keep My commandments, (32) Then I will punish their transgression with the rod, And their iniquity with stripes."*

In Luke chapter twelve quoted above, the context of this passage of scripture is dealing with those called to the ministry. For our Lord is responding to Peter's question as to whether our Lord is speaking to everyone, or only to the apostles. Notice the great reward that our Lord bestows on His ministry gifts, in that He clearly tells them that on that day, those who are faithful will be made rulers over all He has. But notice also, the judgement pronounced on those who are disobedient. The call to the ministry by the Lord, is not to be taken lightly. Those who do so, do it at their peril. Again, I remind those called to the ministry, that Paul said, "Woe is me if I do not preach the gospel".

# Ministry gifts judgement

Someone said, how is it possible that our Lord will give His servant over to be beaten on that day? Not only is it possible, but our Lord said that this is exactly what awaited those called to the ministry, who chose not to fulfil their ministries. The context of Psalm eighty-nine quoted above, is that God the Father is speaking of the Lord's saints under the new covenant. He tells us that if we break His commandments in this life, that we can expect to be punished with the rod and with stripes. We know from the epistles and the book of Revelation, that when our Lord chastens us in this life, that He does so with tribulation, sickness and even early death. I have no idea what form those stripes will take on that day, but it certainly sounds like a punishment to be avoided at all costs. These scriptures are controversial, and not many teach on them because they make us uncomfortable, but Jesus the Head of the church, taught them and we had better pay attention to them. In the passage of scripture from Luke's gospel, the Lord has placed those called to the ministry, into two categories. The first category, knew that they were called to the ministry but chose not to answer His call, and did not enter the ministry. They deliberately ignored His call. Our Lord said that these would be beaten with many stripes. The second category are those who are not aware that they have been called to the ministry, due to their ignorance in following the leading of the Holy Spirit. As a result, they would be beaten with few stripes. The reason that they would be beaten with few stripes is because they were not deliberately disobedient, but rather disobedient due to ignorance. But notice that because our Lord takes His ministry gifts extremely seriously, they were still beaten. It is also important to note that the one who answers the call of God to enter into the ministry, and then misses his calling, by for example becoming a pastor instead of a prophet, as the Lord may have called him, is not included in this group. And so, they would not therefore be included in the punishment given to these saints. The reason that he would not be punished, is because he has answered his call, he just got his call wrong. In the instance where the minister of God answers his call but gets it wrong, the scripture that we read earlier in one Corinthians chapter three will apply on their day of judgment. Because they had missed God in their true calling, the majority of their works would be burned up on that day, because they would be works done outside of the Lord's perfect will for their ministries.

*Acts 20:26-27 "Therefore I testify to you this day that I am innocent of the blood of all men. (27) For I have not shunned to declare to you the whole counsel of God."*

*2 Timothy 1:15 "This you know, that all those in Asia have turned away from me, among whom are Phygellus and Hermogenes."*

*3 John 1:9-10 "I wrote to the church, but Diotrephes, who loves to have the pre-eminence among them, does not receive us. (10) Therefore, if I come, I will call to mind his deeds which he does, prating against us with malicious words. And not content with that, he himself does not receive the brethren, and forbids those who wish to, putting them out of the church."*

# Ministry gifts judgement

*Ezekiel 3:20 "Again, when a righteous man turns from his righteousness and commits iniquity, and I lay a stumbling block before him, he shall die; because you did not give him warning, he shall die in his sin, and his righteousness which he has done shall not be remembered; but his blood I will require at your hand."*

Something else that ministers of the gospel need to be aware of, is the content of the gospel that they preach and teach. In Acts chapter twenty quoted above, the apostle Paul stated that God would not hold him to account for the blood of others on that day. The reason he could say this was because he had not been selective in what he taught, with regards to the gospel of God. He taught the whole counsel of God, even if certain parts were not popular. In fact, Paul was so diligent in teaching the full counsel of God that towards the end of his ministry, there were many churches that would not allow him to preach in their churches anymore. Paul, in writing to Timothy in two Timothy chapter one quoted above, tells us that he was no longer welcome to preach in the churches of Asia, even though he had planted many of those same churches. I am fully convinced that if the apostle Paul were alive today, that there are many churches today that would not let Paul anywhere near their pulpits. Because the gospel that he teaches in his epistles, is far too uncomfortable for many in the church today. In third John chapter one quoted above, we see that the apostle John had the same problem towards the end of his ministry, in that there were certain churches where he and his ministry team were no longer welcome. The whole counsel of God as taught to us in His gospel, is not a popular gospel among carnal believers. Those called to the ministry and who refuse to teach certain truths of the gospel, because those parts may upset the hearers or may affect their offerings, will have to give an account to their Master on that day. Paul said that if he did not teach the whole counsel of God and one who heard him stumbled because they were unaware of the truth, then God would hold him accountable for their blood. The Lord taught this same principle to the ministry gifts under the old covenant as well. In Ezekiel chapter three quoted above, God warned the prophet of this very thing, by telling him that if the Lord's prophets did not warn the righteous man to not turn from righteousness, that when they stumbled, that the Lord would hold the prophet accountable. So, what does the Lord mean when He says that He will require their blood at the hands of the minister, that does not warn the righteous (or the wicked for the matter)? I don't know, but I certainly don't want to find out and so by the grace of God, I choose to be like Paul, and declare the full counsel of God.

*Luke 12:41-46 "Then Peter said to Him, "Lord, do You speak this parable only to us, or to all people?" (42) And the Lord said, "Who then is that faithful and wise steward, whom his master will make ruler over his household, to give them their portion of food in due season? ... (45) But if that servant says in his heart, 'My master is delaying his coming,' and begins to beat the male and female servants, and to eat and drink and be drunk, (46) the master of that servant will come on a day when he is not looking for him, and at an hour when he is not aware, and will cut him in two and appoint him his portion with the unbelievers."*

*Philippians 3:17-19 "Brethren, join in following my example, and note those who so walk, as you have us for a pattern. (18) For many walk, of whom I have told you often, and now tell you even weeping, that they are the enemies of the cross of Christ: (19) whose end is destruction, whose god is their belly, and whose glory is in their shame--who set their mind on earthly things."*

*Matthew 25:14-30 "For the kingdom of heaven is like a man traveling to a far country, who called his own servants and delivered his goods to them. (15) And to one he gave five talents, to another two, and to another one, to each according to his own ability; and immediately he went on a journey. (16) Then he who had received the five talents went and traded with them, and made another five talents. (17) And likewise, he who had received two gained two more also. (18) But he who had received one went and dug in the ground, and hid his lord's money. (19) After a long time the lord of those servants came and settled accounts with them. (20) "So, he who had received five talents came and brought five other talents, saying, 'Lord, you delivered to me five talents; look, I have gained five more talents besides them.' (21) His lord said to him, 'Well done, good and faithful servant; you were faithful over a few things, I will make you ruler over many things. Enter into the joy of your lord.' (22) He also who had received two talents came and said, 'Lord, you delivered to me two talents; look, I have gained two more talents besides them.' (23) His lord said to him, 'Well done, good and faithful servant; you have been faithful over a few things, I will make you ruler over many things. Enter into the joy of your lord.' (24) "Then he who had received the one talent came and said, 'Lord, I knew you to be a hard man, reaping where you have not sown, and gathering where you have not scattered seed. (25) And I was afraid, and went and hid your talent in the ground. Look, there you have what is yours.' (26) "But his lord answered and said to him, 'You wicked and lazy servant, you knew that I reap where I have not sown, and gather where I have not scattered seed. (27) So, you ought to have deposited my money with the bankers, and at my coming I would have received back my own with interest. (28) So, take the talent from him, and give it to him who has ten talents. (29) 'For to everyone who has, more will be given, and he will have abundance; but from him who does not have, even what he has will be taken away. (30) And cast the unprofitable servant into the outer darkness. There will be weeping and gnashing of teeth."*

There is one last comment that needs to be made, with regards to the judgment received by the ministry gifts. And that is that the one who abuses their ministry gift, is in danger of being treated as one who commits the sin unto death. In Luke chapter twelve quoted above, our Lord Jesus tells us about some ministry gifts that will have their portion appointed with the unbelievers on that day. In context, we know that our Lord is talking about those called to the ministry, because He makes this clear in verses forty-one and forty-two. So, what behaviour do these ministers display, that causes our Lord to place them with the unbelievers on that day? When the scriptures say that they begin to beat the Lord's servants, the word translated "beat" also means to "offend". These same ministers live hypocritical lifestyles, by living in the flesh and gratifying the lusts of their flesh. In other words, these ministers cause the Lord's servants to become offended, and fall away from following the Lord. In Philippians chapter three quoted above, the apostle Paul is admonishing the church to follow the example of his lifestyle and others like him, as ministers of the gospel. Paul then tells us that he weeps for other ministers of the gospel who were not walking as examples to the flock, for he tells us that their end is destruction. It just may be that when our Lord requires the blood of those who stumble at the hands of His ministers, that He is referring to this statement that He made, in that He will "appoint him his portion with the unbelievers". I will close this chapter with one of the parables that our Lord Jesus taught us regarding the day of judgement. The parable quoted above from Matthew chapter twenty-five, is very similar to the one we looked at earlier in the chapter that dealt with unforgiven sin. Both parables deal with the day of judgement, but although the parables are similar, they deal with two different categories of the Lord's servants. Unlike the first parable, in which every servant received the same amount, in this parable the servants are given different amounts based on their abilities. The first parable dealt with all the Lord's saints, whereas in this parable our Lord is dealing with His ministry gifts. The outcome in both parables for the ones who did not use their talents is almost identical, in that both have their inheritance taken from them. But in the parable dealing with the Lord's ministry gifts, the judgement pronounced is far more serious, because they are banished to outer darkness for all eternity. For to whom much has been committed, of him they will ask the more.

# Chapter 7

# Unbelievers' eternal judgement

## The second resurrection

*Revelation 20:5-15 "But the rest of the dead did not live again until the thousand years were finished. This is the first resurrection. … (11) Then I saw a great white throne and Him who sat on it, from whose face the earth and the heaven fled away. And there was found no place for them. (12) And I saw the dead, small and great, standing before God, and books were opened. And another book was opened, which is the Book of Life. And the dead were judged according to their works, by the things which were written in the books. (13) The sea gave up the dead who were in it, and Death and Hades delivered up the dead who were in them. And they were judged, each one according to his works. (14) Then Death and Hades were cast into the lake of fire. This is the second death. (15) And anyone not found written in the Book of Life was cast into the lake of fire."*

*John 5:28-29 "Do not marvel at this; for the hour is coming in which all who are in the graves will hear His voice (29) and come forth-- those who have done good, to the resurrection of life, and those who have done evil, to the resurrection of condemnation."*

*John 3:18 "He who believes in Him is not condemned; but he who does not believe is condemned already, because he has not believed in the name of the only begotten Son of God."*

*Acts 13:46 "Then Paul and Barnabas grew bold and said, "It was necessary that the word of God should be spoken to you first; but since you reject it, and judge yourselves unworthy of everlasting life, behold, we turn to the Gentiles."*

All unbelievers will incur the judgment of God, at the second resurrection. As you will recall, we saw earlier that the saints' judgement will take place at the first resurrection. Scripture in Revelations chapter twenty quoted above, reveals to us that the rest of the dead will not be raised at that time. The judgement of all unbelievers will take place after the thousand-year reign of Christ on the earth. It will be at that time that all unbelievers will be raised from the dead, to stand before the great white throne of God. At this resurrection, our Lord Jesus has taught us that all unbelievers are already condemned even before they are judged, for He calls it the resurrection of condemnation. In John chapter five quoted above, our Lord refers to the two resurrections. The first one, He calls the resurrection of life, which is the resurrection of His saints. And the second one, He calls the resurrection of condemnation, which is the resurrection of all the unbelievers. The reason that they would have already been condemned, is because all who do not believe the gospel are condemned by default, for they condemn themselves. This truth is revealed to us by our Lord Jesus in John's gospel chapter three, as quoted above. In Acts chapter thirteen quoted above, the Holy Spirit speaking through the apostle Paul, tells unbelievers who reject the gospel of Jesus Christ, that they judge themselves unworthy of eternal life, not God. And so, the unbelievers will already stand condemned at this judgement, but what remains to be judged will be their works, in order to determine what their eternal punishment will be. This is the reason why the books will be opened, for those books have recorded every detail of every unbelievers' life.

## The saints will judge

*John 5:22-27 "For the Father judges no one, but has committed all judgment to the Son, ... (27) and has given Him authority to execute judgment also, because He is the Son of Man."*

*1 Corinthians 6:2 "Do you not know that the saints will judge the world? And if the world will be judged by you, are you unworthy to judge the smallest matters?"*

*Matthew 12:41-42 "The men of Nineveh will rise up in the judgment with this generation and condemn it, because they repented at the preaching of Jonah; and indeed, a greater than Jonah is here. (42) The queen of the South will rise up in the judgment with this generation and condemn it, for she came from the ends of the earth to hear the wisdom of Solomon; and indeed, a greater than Solomon is here."*

*Revelation 3:9 "Indeed I will make those of the synagogue of Satan, who say they are Jews and are not, but lie--indeed I will make them come and worship before your feet, and to know that I have loved you."*

As revealed to us in John chapter five quoted above, God the Father has committed all judgement to His Son, Jesus Christ our Lord. The reason that our Father did that, is because Jesus the Son of God, is also the Son of Man. And as such, He is fully qualified to judge all men, for He lived as a man, who never committed any sin. As we have already seen, our Lord Jesus has reserved the judgement of His saints, for Himself. But He has committed the judgement of the unbelievers, to His saints. In one Corinthians chapter six quoted above, the Holy Spirit through the apostle Paul, revealed this truth to us when He wrote to the church telling them that we will judge the world. In Matthew chapter twelve quoted above, our Lord Jesus also confirmed this truth to us, when He taught on what it would be like in the day of the unbelievers' judgement. For our Lord Jesus taught us that the men of Nineveh and the queen of Sheba would be among those who would pronounce judgement on the generation that heard Jesus preach in the flesh, but rejected Him. The men of Nineveh and the queen of Sheba are among the saints in heaven today, for their faith was accounted to them for righteousness. In Revelation chapter three quoted above, our Lord Jesus told the church at Philadelphia that He would one day make their adversaries come and worship before their feet. It will be on this day of judgement when this will happen. The unbelievers that we have known in our lives and who mocked our belief in Jesus Christ as our Saviour, will be made to come and worship at our feet as we pronounce eternal judgement on them. As an aside, this is one of the reasons that believers who practiced a life of sin, will not participate in the inheritance to reign with Christ, and will only be saved. For God is not a hypocrite, and He will not allow one of His children who practiced sin in their life, to then sit and judge unbelievers for those same sins.

*Romans 2:16 "in the day when God will judge the secrets of men by Jesus Christ, according to my gospel."*

*1 Timothy 5:24 "Some men's sins are clearly evident, preceding them to judgment, but those of some men follow later."*

*1 Corinthians 6:3 "Do you not know that we shall judge angels? How much more, things that pertain to this life?"*

*Matthew 25:41 "Then He will also say to those on the left hand, 'Depart from Me, you cursed, into the everlasting fire prepared for the devil and his angels."*

Based on what is recorded in the books that are opened, each unbeliever will receive differing degrees of punishment. We will judge the secrets of men's hearts on that day, for their secrets will be revealed in the books that are opened. In Romans chapter two quoted above, the Holy Spirit through the apostle Paul, reveals this truth to us. This is why Paul states in one Timothy chapter five quoted above, that we can clearly see the sins of some of men in this life, but then there are those who look good on the outside, but inwardly they are just as sinful. Their sins will not be hidden on that day, for all will be revealed. However, not only will the saints judge the world at this time, but we will also judge Satan's angels, as revealed to us by the apostle Paul, in one Corinthians chapter six quoted above. The church will not judge Satan himself, for he has already been judged, as revealed to us by our Lord in John chapter sixteen. The lake of fire and brimstone, which is the second death, was always prepared for Satan and his angels. God never intended that man should end up there. In Matthew chapter twenty-five quoted above, our Lord Jesus reveals to us that the lake of fire was always intended for Satan and his angels. But sadly, most of mankind have chosen to follow after the prince of the power of the air, and become sons of disobedience. And so, they too will be cast into the lake of fire and brimstone to suffer for all eternity.

**There are degrees of punishment**

*Psalms 88:6-7 "You have laid me in the lowest pit, In darkness, in the depths. (7) Your wrath lies heavy upon me, And You have afflicted me with all Your waves."*

*Isaiah 14:12-15 "How you are fallen from heaven, O Lucifer, son of the morning! How you are cut down to the ground, you who weakened the nations! (13) For you have said in your heart: 'I will ascend into heaven, I will exalt my throne above the stars of God; I will also sit on the mount of the congregation on the farthest sides of the north; (14) I will ascend above the heights of the clouds, I will be like the Most High.' (15) Yet you shall be brought down to Sheol, To the lowest depths of the Pit."*

*Luke 10:10-12 "But whatever city you enter, and they do not receive you, go out into its streets and say, (11) 'The very dust of your city which clings to us we wipe off against you. Nevertheless, know this, that the kingdom of God has come near you.' (12) But I say to you that it will be more tolerable in that Day for Sodom than for that city."*

*Luke 11:24-26 "When an unclean spirit goes out of a man, he goes through dry places, seeking rest; and finding none, he says, 'I will return to my house from which I came.' (25) And when he comes, he finds it swept and put in order. (26) Then he goes and takes with him seven other spirits more wicked than himself, and they enter and dwell there; and the last state of that man is worse than the first."*

Hell, is made up of many different levels. The lower down one is placed in hell, the greater the degree of punishment that is incurred there. Our Lord Jesus was laid in the lowest pit of hell to suffer the wrath of God for our sins. In Psalm eighty-eight quoted above, the Holy Spirit reveals this truth to us through the psalmist prophesying the words of our Lord Jesus, when He was in the depths of the earth for three days and nights. We also know that Satan will be locked up in the lowest pit of hell during the thousand-year reign of Christ. For in Isaiah chapter fourteen quoted above, the Holy Spirit reveals that truth to us. The lake of fire and brimstone will be similar to hades, from the point of view of having different levels to it. And again, the lower the level in that lake of fire, the higher the degree of eternal punishment that will be incurred there. Our Lord Jesus revealed this truth to us in Luke chapter ten quoted above, when He taught on the punishment that will be incurred on that day. Our Lord taught us that for example, it will be more tolerable for the city of Sodom than the city of Capernaum. The reason for that is because the citizens of Sodom will not be cast down to the same depth in the lake, as the citizens of Capernaum, on that day. Even in Satan's kingdom, there are differing levels of wickedness among his angels, or demons if you will. Our Lord Jesus revealed that truth to us in Luke chapter eleven quoted above, when He spoke about Satan's kingdom. For our Lord told us that this particular demon went and found seven other demons that were more wicked than himself. And so, as there are varying degrees of wickedness among Satan's angels, so there are also varying degrees of wickedness among the sons of men. Based on the wickedness of the individual being judged, the saints will pronounce on them their eternal judgement. We have already seen that Satan will be committed to the lowest pit of hell, while he is locked up during the millennial reign of Christ. So, it is plainly evident that he will be committed to the lowest level in the lake of fire, for all eternity. His angels will then receive their judgements, based on their wickedness revealed on that day.

*2 Corinthians 11:13-15 "For such are false apostles, deceitful workers, transforming themselves into apostles of Christ. (14) And no wonder! For Satan, himself transforms himself into an angel of light. (15) Therefore, it is no great thing if his ministers also transform themselves into ministers of righteousness, whose end will be according to their works."*

*Hebrews 10:29 "Of how much worse punishment, do you suppose, will he be thought worthy who has trampled the Son of God underfoot, counted the blood of the covenant by which he was sanctified a common thing, and insulted the Spirit of grace?"*

*Revelation 14:9-11 "Then a third angel followed them, saying with a loud voice, "If anyone worships the beast and his image, and receives his mark on his forehead or on his hand, (10) he himself shall also drink of the wine of the wrath of God, which is poured out full strength into the cup of His indignation. He shall be tormented with fire and brimstone in the presence of the holy angels and in the presence of the Lamb. (11) And the smoke of their torment ascends forever and ever; and they have no rest day or night, who worship the beast and his image, and whoever receives the mark of his name."*

*Isaiah 66:22-24 "For as the new heavens and the new earth Which I will make shall remain before Me," says the LORD, "So shall your descendants and your name remain. (23) And it shall come to pass That from one New Moon to another, and from one*

# Unbelievers' eternal judgement

*Sabbath to another, all flesh shall come to worship before Me," says the LORD.  (24)  "And they shall go forth and look Upon the corpses of the men Who have transgressed against Me. For their worm does not die, and their fire is not quenched. They shall be an abhorrence to all flesh."*

Among the sons of men, scripture reveals to us the different levels of wickedness, as viewed by heaven. Those who will experience the worst punishment in that day, are those who are Satan's ministers. These are the false teachers and false prophets, as mentioned in two Corinthians chapter eleven above. For these deliberately teach false doctrine in the church, in order to mislead the church. The next level of punishment will be reserved for the ones who have at one time been believers saved by grace, who have since turned their backs on Jesus and no longer follow Him. Hebrews chapter ten quoted above, describes these individuals as having counted the blood of the covenant a common thing. The next level of punishment will be reserved for those who have followed after the Antichrist and worshipped him. This is revealed to us in Revelation chapter fourteen quoted above. After them, there will be those who have rejected the preaching of the gospel in order to be saved. We have already seen in Luke chapter ten quoted earlier, that these individuals will incur a greater degree of punishment on that day. It is truly a dangerous thing to be exposed to the gospel, and believers who share the gospel with others, should keep this in mind. The next level of punishment will be reserved for the truly wicked, like the citizens of Sodom and Gomorrah. And finally, the rest of the unbelievers will receive their judgement. All not found recorded in the

Book of Life, will be condemned to eternal punishment in the lake of fire.      The lake of fire and brimstone will be present outside the new Jerusalem throughout all eternity, for all to see. For scripture tells us that the lake of fire will be in the presence of the holy angels and the Lamb. And we will see the smoke of their torment ascending forever. The Holy Spirit confirms this truth to us through the prophet Isaiah, when He tells us that those who come up to worship before the Lord in the new Jerusalem, will go forth to look at those who are suffering their eternal punishment, in the lake of fire and brimstone.

# If you believe you can receive Jesus as your Lord and Saviour by praying this prayer

Dear Heavenly Father,

I come to You in the Name of Jesus.

Your Word says, "the one who comes to Me I will by no means cast out" (John 6:37), so I know You won't cast me out, but You take me in and I thank You for it. You said in Your Word, "Whoever calls on the name of the lord shall be saved." (Romans 10:13). I am calling on Your Name, so I know that You save me right now. You also said, "If you confess with your mouth the Lord Jesus and believe in your heart that God has raised Him from the dead, you will be saved. (10) For with the heart one believes unto righteousness, and with the mouth confession is made unto salvation" (Romans 10:9-10). I believe in my heart Jesus Christ is the Son of God. I believe that He was raised from the dead for my justification, and I confess Him now as my Lord. Because Your Word says, "with the heart one believes unto righteousness," and I do believe with my heart, I have now become the righteousness of God in Christ Jesus (2 Cor. 5:21) . . .

And I am now saved!

Thank You, Lord!

Welcome to the family of God. Now that you are His child you need to read your bible (especially the New Testament) daily, spend time in prayer daily and join a local church that will teach you to be filled with the Holy Spirit with the evidence of speaking in other tongues, so that you can grow spiritually. You also need to tell others how Jesus has saved you so that they too can be saved.

# About the Author

From childhood, Michael E.B. Maher has always known that the Lord's call was upon his life for the ministry. When he was saved at the age of twenty-two, almost immediately the Lord Jesus began to deal with him about entering the ministry. He went to Oral Roberts University to enrol but circumstances prevented him from following that path. After a period, the call for the ministry once again became very strong, and finally in the early 1990's Michael entered the ministry. After a period, he left the ministry and went into the business world. Although he experienced success in the business world, he was outside of the Lord's will for his life. Over time, he began to drift from the close relationship with the Lord that he had always known. By 2010 the Lord's patience had run out, and Michael suffered his first series of heart attacks. By this time, Michael had become so worldly in his thinking that it never even occurred to him that the Lord had begun to judge him for his disobedience. After his medical treatment, Michael went back into his career thinking that all was back on track again. But now the Lord started to unravel his career as well. Whereas before he had always excelled in his work, he now found completely dissatisfied with what he was doing. And so, at the height of his career he decided to take early retirement. It was during this time that his relationship with the Lord grew again. Although the Lord had brought him to this point, he was still not in the Lord's will. And so, Michael then had his next series of heart attacks. It was only now that the Lord finally got his attention and he committed to the Lord that if He would spare his life, that he would finally answer the Lord's call to the ministry. And so, in 2014 Michael Maher Ministries was begun. From the beginning, the mandate given to Michael from the Lord Jesus was to preach the word. And so, this ministry preaches the word of God on every available platform around the world.

# Michael Maher Ministries

## *Free Subscription*

Join hundreds of others from countries around the world and read our Daily Bible Teaching Email and more, that will help you to grow in your walk with the Lord Jesus.

*Thank you so much for your dedication and commitment. These daily teachings are invaluable to me and my family.*
*Kind regards*

*-Bill Watt-Pringle*

*Hi Michael*
*Thanx so much for this word, it really struck home. It's now helping me to get my act together*
*Sue*

- *Suzanne Honeyborne*

*Thank u for explaining. Your messages are very helpful to keep reading & renewing my mind*

- *Alison Joy Kruger Hale*

Log on to our website to subscribe.

www.mebmm.org

# Michael Maher Ministries

## *Online Bible Courses*

Our courses are designed to help believers grow in their faith and reach their full potential in Christ that God intended for their lives, through the study of His word.

## *Flexible*

Enrol any time: choose your topic of study; study at your own pace.

## *Affordable*

Pay as you go.

Log on to our website to register.

www.mebmm.org

# Michael Maher Ministries

13 Windsor Lodge
Beach Road
Fish Hoek, 7974
Cape Town
South Africa
Phone: +27 082-974-3599

## On the Web

www.mebmm.org